AMERICA IN CRISIS

MAKING THINGS RIGHT
IN A NATION GONE WRONG

BY  JIM BOHANNON

America In Crisis: Making Things Right in a Nation Gone Wrong

Copyright © 2000 Jim Bohannon

FIRST EDITION
ISBN: 1-879706-9-38
LC: 00 135266

Design: Corinna Wilborn, www.grapheon.com, © 2000

TO MY BEAUTIFUL, LOVELY WIFE, ANNABELLE

This work would never have seen the light of day without the inspiration of Werner Riefling, who saw something in my thoughts worth preserving. Bill Burkett was a font of guidance and patience in helping those thoughts get put on paper. The whole staff at Paper Chase Press probably never before had to do as much paper-chasing, and I thank them for cleaning up after my random procrastinations. At Westwood One, Vice President for News Bart Tessler and Senior Producer Greg Johnson, plus Dennis Maccarthy and Jane Hautanen have provided the consistent support which has made this project a pleasure. And special thanks goes to my wife, Annabelle, for her wise counsel and unceasing encouragement. Any faults or flaws herein should be vested in the appropriate person — me.

TABLE OF CONTENTS

> *Civility doesn't start with imposition of some outside code, or substitution of laws to govern public behavior for the old religious monoliths, not in my opinion. Civility starts with a personal decision not to play by the ugly rules, not to escalate. Civility starts with you and me following our own ethical code in the face of the pressures of the day.*

> *We no longer have a clear, unified vision of exactly what we want our children to learn. We are floundering, because we have either forgotten who we as a culture are, or we're so interested in our individual gains, we adopt a "can't see the forest for the trees" mentality. As long as the weather's good on this side of the block, we can ignore what it means to be "we the people."*

> *If Prohibition taught us anything, it should have been that in a free nation, where there is an overwhelming public acceptance of a particular activity, it is fruitless to try to prohibit that activity. The more Draconian the measures employed in the attempt to stop the activity, the more creative become the efforts to circumvent those measures. At the same time, respect for the law and its enforcers wanes quickly. You can take prohibition only so far in a free society.*

> *Where I would like to draw the line is in the "how" of advertising, in which canny behaviorists plot campaigns designed to make us feel life is just not worth living without designer jeans, cell phones and hot tubs. Every supplier of goods is competing fiercely for an after-all finite number of dollars from we the consumers, and increasingly that competition is no-holds-barred.*

> *While there is an element of truth in the rationalizations that politicians offer for maintaining the status quo, they could be freed of those bonds by realistic campaign reform. But I'm betting it won't happen anytime soon, not until the American public has had enough of government by checkbook and stands up on its hind legs.*

> *I think that now would be exactly the wrong time in history to indulge in political isolationism. We cannot let the financial interests, as represented by border-spanning mega-corporations, lay the ground rules for global economy. We as Americans must support a government that is willing to actively get involved across the world.*

> *It is my opinion that much of the resistance to severe punishment for the guilty is a widespread distrust of those administer it. Unfortunately, much of that distrust has a basis in fact. The police and prosecutors appear to see their jobs as a matter of clearing cases as fast as possible. In such a hurried atmosphere, mistakes multiply.*

“ Stations that try to report news of note—serious news, news that requires perhaps some thought of the listener or viewer—typically wind up third or fourth in the ratings race, beaten by Wheel of Fortune. The force-feeding of information needed for an informed citizenship simply is not popular. ”

“ Democracy, I believe, is like a close friendship. You develop a close friendship, and always manage to find time out of your busy schedules to keep the friendship green. Then something happens— one moves away, or work becomes all-demanding. Maybe a good period of time goes by, and one day you pick up the phone out of the blue and call your friend, fully expecting to slide back into the warm natural rhythm of two minds in synch on many things. ”

A M E R I C A

Radios
T.V. shows
Fill my holes
With your goodies

I sold my privacy
So that I would always be pretty
And I can tell you that the best things are free
With proof of purchase

Chorus: Ooo, America, Ooo, America

Pay no more
Attention to the things that you stand for
Sit back, relax, enjoy the war
From your living room

Holocaust
And cable at a fraction of the cost
And just to make sure you don't get lost
Here's the media, media, media, media

Chorus

I embrace your legacy—
The models and the apathy
I know the late night network commonwealth
Is there to help me help myself

All I know
Is my lonely soul
And the remote control

Chorus
—BREE SHARP
FROM HER ALBUM *A CHEAP AND EVIL GIRL*

Preface

IN 1981, WHEN I WAS THE NIGHT SHOW RADIO-TALK HOST FOR WESTWOOD ONE, I was in Chicago for a convention and did a remote broadcast from WCFL, Jim Bohannon's station.

While I was there, I borrowed Pat Keene as my engineer. A real nice guy, by the way.

Anyway, during the course of the program, Pat is telling me about this guy, Jim Bohannon. He went on and on about what a great guy he was, what a great broadcaster he was, and all this. I was so impressed, I tucked Jim's name in the back of head somewhere thinking, "What the heck, you never know when you need a good fill-in." Though normally, in those days, I just called upon the services of the very capable Jim Slade.

It was later in the year, about November of '81, when I had another commitment and Slade is tied up down at Cape Canaveral covering a rocket launch, and he can't get back in time to do the show because a mechanic left a wrench or something in the rocket, and the launch is delayed. I'm in a bit of a spot, so, I think, "Who's good? What about this Jim Bohannon guy?"

Well, it must have been fate or something, because it happened that this Bohannon guy is in Washington D.C. covering a convention. We tracked him down and asked him to sit in for me on the show. The guest that night was the great and inimitable Pierre Salinger. This is a big buy, you know. You really can't just have anyone do the interview. But I think, "What the heck, let's give this Bohannon a chance."

Well, what can I say, Jim was terrific. He's a consummate professional. Very polished, but personable and likeable. And that voice! He's got a terrific radio voice. So, pretty much from that point forward, Jim was my fill-in guy. Eventually, I go to television, CNN. To me, Jim Bohannon was the best man to take over my show at Westwood One. And to this day, he's still one of the top radio performers in the country. I knew we had a winner here.

In the meantime, I have had Jim as a guest on Larry King Live when I want to have his unique view on things. He's very knowledgeable. Has his fingers on the pulse of what's going on in this country. Very in tune. He has a calm, reasoned, logical approach to today's issues. He's the guy you go to when you want a balanced opinion. The other thing about Jim is that he's sincere, genuine. He loves what he does, and he is good at it. And I believe he considers it his job to help people in this country see things as they are, and find a way to deal with today's challenges.

Which brings me to Jim's book. Jim is right. There are a lot of great things about our country. He loves his country as much as I do. And he's very concerned about the welfare of our fellow Americans.

But he also sees that there are some real challenges we face.

He is very concerned about the future of our kids, for example. He wants everyone to learn more about this country's history, to be better informed, to be better educated, and to participate in the political process and the business of governing our country.

He wants families to succeed in having happy and balanced lives, so our kids have an even brighter future than ourselves. He's concerned about things like crime and drugs. He's even concerned about how we in the media conduct ourselves, and the way we influence our listeners, our viewers, our readers — everyone.

Jim Bohannon is not just some guy who just wants to gripe and complain about the not so good things. He looks for a way to resolve things, to make things better, and he believes that building on the strength of American ideas which made this country great is the way to go about it. He speaks from his heart, and from his mind.

I believe Jim Bohannon has much to say, and this book is a good place for him to get his point across. And he does a great job. Everyone should get a copy.

I wish Jim all the best in all he does, including this book.

All My Best,
Larry King

Introduction

HELLO, I'M JIM BOHANNON. I've been opening radio broadcasts with some variation of that statement since I first went on the air on my hometown radio station in Lebanon, Missouri, in 1960.

I was 16 years old, and the bright lights and big mikes of network radio were the farthest thing from my mind when I stopped by the station to pick up some newswire "copy" for a high school class assignment.

But I quickly realized during that visit that if I were on the air, and the wind was right, I could be heard up and down Main Street. It seemed like a great way to reach my true goal: meeting girls. Not the noblest of motives, but it worked out—I actually did meet girls.

The station's call letters were KLWT (I always said they stood for: "Keep Listening, We're Trying") and I was a disk jockey playing the popular tunes of the day.

News was not yet a staple of the radio business when I began, but they did have periodic news broadcasts for me to perform as part of my duties.

This was known as the "rip and read" school of journalism: heavy electric teletypewriters chugged steadily, printing stories from around the world onto a roll of tractor feed paper, similar to early computer tractor-feeds. You could "rip" off a sheet that contained each story by using the edge of the plexiglass face plate set into the front of the machine's dust cover. Minutes after scanning the "copy" and digesting its contents, a DJ was expected to be on the air reading the latest news into the microphone.

I had no voice training whatsoever. I was a long way then from what I like to consider my dulcet tones of today. My boss, Jack Sellers, was a good guy and something of a wit. He would say to me "I'd pay you what you're worth — but it would be illegal." The minimum wage then was a dollar an hour.

My second radio gig was in Springfield, Mo., where I attended college at Southwestern Missouri State University. This station had the "cool" call sign KICK, and was heavily into rock-n-roll: Elvis, the Beatles, the whole music of the 60s. One of the things that sticks in my mind about that period is a 1964 trip that another DJ and I took with three busloads of excited kids to see the Beatles in Kansas City. I actually met and interviewed the Fab Four.

My voice had changed by then from its halting Midwestern twang on the air — but still was far from smooth. I guess the best way I can characterize my presentation then is that I was a screaming disk jockey. That kind of over-the-top delivery was very popular then.

Getting Into The News

To be perfectly honest, the music of those times began to wear on me. The charm of being a DJ was replaced by a growing interest in news. I already had gotten tired of thinking up 28 ways to say: "And here are the Doors!" I went to KWTO (also in Springfield) to do more news.

Little by little, my voice smoothed out and I was able to sound more professional, without benefit of any formal voice training or breath lessons.

One of the highlights of working at KWTO was when I got to chase a real, live tornado. Exciting stuff for a young radio journalist. I was drawn along in its wake almost irresistibly, trying to catch up with it— and I almost did, too. What I did get was great eyewitness tape from people still rattled from their near-miss. Now that was lots more exciting than spinning rock 'n roll records.

My Military Stint

Then my college deferment ran out. And many of you who came of age in the 1960s will know what that means: I ended up in the Army.

In my case, I was assigned to the Army Security Agency and spent one year of my time in Vietnam, including a little skirmish called the Tet Offensive. Eventually, before my Army tour was over, I was transferred to a post near Washington, D.C., and was able to work part-time at WTOP, an all-news station there. I also worked at WRC.

I stayed in Washington after military separation, because there's an awful lot of news always happening in the nation's capital. My last flirtation with disk-jockey status was when WPGC there courted me to be part of an overnight rock 'n roll tag team to be known as "Famous Amos and Handy Andy." Even within the Beltway, rock 'n roll was still hot.

I would have been Handy Andy.

Newsman For Life

When I turned the job down, the die was cast. I was a newsman from then on. It was while broadcasting for WTOP that I achieved my "personal best" for continuous on-air time during a breaking news story.

I spent 21 straight hours at the microphone, coordinating coverage of a takeover of the top floor of city hall by a group of Hanafi Muslims. They also occupied the B'Nai B'rith offices and the Islamic Center. It was an armed takeover, violent; one man was killed. The tension was nerve-wracking. They were angered at a movie they thought disrespectful of Allah, and it was my impression they threw in the B'nai B'rith takeover for good measure because they disliked Jews on general principles. When I finally turned over the mike, I was limp as the proverbial dishrag. It was exciting, but it was an exhausting experience.

A happier D.C. memory occurred in 1977, which blended aspects of news coverage and talk-show radio.

I was in the studio and on the air when Muhammad Ali chose to make one of his unscheduled personal appearances in a neighborhood, dancing and weaving, kidding the residents along, inventing snippets of rhyme as only he could do. He was at the height of his powers, in town for a fight. Someone from the neighborhood got on a pay phone to alert my station to this bit of breaking news. I told the caller to go tell Ali he had a guy on the phone who could sell a lot of tickets to his fight.

Ali was a great showman, and he immediately saw the opportunity for what it was. He came right to the phone booth, and I put him on the air. He was in fine fettle, and the interview was full of fun.

I bet we did sell a lot of tickets, too.

Larry King

In March of 1980, I moved to WCFL in Chicago as co-host, with my then-wife Camille, of the morning news block. That was where station engineer Pat Keene set events in motion which would redirect the whole course of my life.

Larry King was already famous. He had blown into the Windy City for a remote broadcast from our facility and borrowed Keene as his engineer. During breaks in the broadcast, Pat kept telling Larry how wonderful I was. Then, sometime later, while I happened to be passing through Washington D.C., the King people called and asked if I could sit in for Larry. Well, obviously, I did. I interviewed Pierre Salinger. Looking back on that first night hosting a network program with a famous guest, I guess you could say it was like learning to swim in the middle of the English Channel—and in public. The rest, as they say, is history.

For the next 11 years I was Larry King's regular backup.

In January of 1993, Larry moved to television. At first he was doing both CNN and his night radio show; then CNN and an afternoon show; and finally just CNN. The nighttime radio spot became mine.

Larry is a good friend and an inspiration. He is an inspired talk show host and interviewer.

This Book

One of the many wonderful things about our country is our freedom of expression. I'm so enthusiastic about this, that I founded the National Freedom of Information Day, an idea that I first suggested to the board of the Society of Professional Journalists at their national convention in New York City in 1979. Freedom of Information Day is observed each March 16th, on the birthday of James Madison, father of the Bill of Rights, and a particular favorite of mine among the Founding Fathers.

Now, with this book, I enter into another wonderful area of expression and the delivery of information: publishing.

I find myself slightly amazed that my radio career now spans over 40 years now and counting. I have been privileged to rub shoulders with some of the most interesting and newsworthy people in the world as a result of my talk-show work, from statesmen to authors. It has also been my great privilege to associate, through the medium of my radio talk show, with hundreds of thoughtful Americans from all walks of life.

A recurring theme throughout my talk-show career has been that of the troubles besetting America today, as we enter this new century. This book is my attempt to distill some of that information, identify major problems, and offer solutions, or at least ideas, for dealing with them.

This is a great nation, and I have truly been blessed in my career, which now has opened up this opportunity of publishing my thoughts and concerns. I hope this book provides food for thought in helping keep us, as a nation, first among equals in this unruly old world of ours.

Jim Bohannon
MONTGOMERY COUNTY, MD.

CHAPTER 1

Incivility

I AM A LIFELONG FAN OF ALL THINGS AMERICAN, and have always been quick to point out all the things that I think are right about this grand nation of ours. But in over forty years in radio journalism, I have watched with growing unease as the social fabric of our lives has seemed more and more to be unraveling. From children killing children in order to possess an expensive pair of sneakers to "road rage," where adult motorists engage in deadly duels behind the wheel, something's gone wrong, horribly wrong.

My intent in this book is to look at a number of different issues which I find deeply troubling, and where I can, to offer some potentials for solving those issues and turning the United States back onto a more positive course as this new century progresses.

Where to begin?

Our educational system is a shambles, justice is often for sale to the highest bidder, and politics—which should be the life's blood of a representative form of government—is almost a dirty word. Family structures are dissolving under societal stress, our streets are awash with illegal drugs, and special interests seem to dominate every public debate. Extremists for this or that cause fill our ears and eyes with increasingly strident demands for our attention and support. Most of us don't even seem to like each other very much anymore. We certainly seem to feel common everyday decency and civility to be unnecessary.

That last point is where I'd like to begin. After years of thought and consideration, I tend toward the notion that the first thread that began to pull loose from our close-knit national fabric was the fundamental art of being nice to each other.

I well remember when I first noticed blatant public disrespect put on display, and the shock I felt when I witnessed it.

I grew up in a rural area about 30 miles from the Lake of the Ozarks, a premiere Midwest tourist attraction, with its hundreds of miles of shoreline and fish-filled waters. Like most rural Midwesterners, the fundamentals of courtesy were drilled into me from the time I can remember. Courtesies like "please" and "thank you" were commonplace, and I would have no more considered calling a neighboring adult by his first name than flying to the moon on waterwings. Respect of others was a given, not even questioned.

My father was a travelling salesman in the region, and I got to accompany him on his rounds. This exposed me to other areas, and to some of the millions of tourists upon whom the region depended for its financial well being. Most of these folks, though they may have had newer cars or better clothing or different modes of speech, came across as perfectly decent, amiable people.

But not all.

Dr. Jekyll and Mr. Tourist

I can remember my dismay when some mild mannered Dr. Jekyll would turn into Mr. Tourist. Mr. Tourist seemed to have swallowed a bitter draught: he'd use actually profanity in public, even in front of women, and kids like me. The target of their foul mouth would often be local waiters, clerks or gas station attendants. I didn't know big words like "patronizing" then, but I could feel the weight of their scorn and contempt for us bumpkins, and it hurt.

These buffoons would casually toss trash out of their cars and let their children run roughshod through business establishments and resorts, and woe betide the local who attempted to stop the juvenile pillage with a mild rebuke.

These types of tourists, camera-bedecked, Bermuda-shorted and flower-shirted, were the first people I ever saw pick their noses in public.

Before it became almost the national pastime it is today.

I still remember a loud-shirted couple in a big gaudy Cadillac who verbally abused a store clerk because they didn't understand his directions to the lake attraction they were seeking. The words they left floating behind them singed the air blue. The least awful thing they called the clerk was "hillbilly."

Before too long, I associated that boorish behavior with tourists. They seemed to be saying: "hey, we're away from home. None of these yokels will ever see us again. We don't HAVE to be civilized."

By my first definition, then, an awful lot of Americans these days act like perpetual tourists. They all seem to have come to the conclusion that boorish behavior has no consequences, and act accordingly. As if the simple act of exercising civility for its own sake is somehow beyond their thought processes.

Alienation

Maybe this is because we feel so alienated from one another today. Many of us live in the anonymous huddles of the vast metropolitan areas. In the exurbs and suburbs, whole neighborhoods lie vacant during the day because the occupants are off at work. If you still live in a small town or friendly neighborhood of a city, where people know each other and are happy about it, count yourself lucky. The frantic pace of today's world is taking its toll in stress, and one of the casualties is the time it takes to be polite to each other.

Just getting back and forth to work has become not only unpleasant, but dangerous. Road rage has become a documented fact of modern existence. We have airplane rage now, too. And cell phone rage. I haven't heard the term commuter train rage yet, but I'm pretty sure that there are unpleasant or even awful incidents on commuter trains. And city bus drivers across the nation have been abused and even assaulted from time to time, or their passengers have tangled it up with profanity, fists, and sometimes weapons.

I have read some postulations that overcrowded conditions trigger the irritation factor: that human beings simply are not hard-wired to deal with so many of their fellows on such a daily and up-close-and-personal basis. Up-close-and-personal, and yet—anonymous to the other fella. I see the ghost of Mr. Tourist from my boyhood, in his baggy shorts, his foul mouth twisted in an epithet. No consequences, no sweat, no civility.

Consequences

Well I'm here to assert there are consequences.

Our entire cohesiveness as a nation threatens to unravel with the display of such self-centered, selfish attitudes.

It was once a homily that all wars had their roots in simple discourtesy; no less an authority than Gibbon, author of *History of the Decline and Fall of the Roman Empire*, looked at such issues. He observed that societies at which Romans sneered as "barbaric" actually had highly developed codes of personal courtesy. In those horse cultures that eventually sacked Rome, every able-bodied man went armed. One did not give offense lightly, for the consequences could be immediate.

Unfortunately, mankind always has seemed to need a reason outside himself to behave. If it wasn't the strong right arm of the other guy, it was some outside "bogeyman": behave or you will die and go to hell. Religious teachings which incorporated civility also incorporated the consequences. Almost every major religion in the world has at its center some version of the Golden Rule: Do unto others as you would have them do unto you. In modern times this has evolved into secular humanism: humane treatment is right because it is its own reward, not a method of laying up brownie points for the afterlife.

For me, I reject the idea of burning bushes and so forth laying down the law to humans and I don't buy supernatural intervention. Just that far, I am in agreement with Mr. Tourist: there aren't necessarily going to be any outside consequences for boorish behavior. (Unless your boorish behavior coincides with the trajectory of somebody who has had enough of it all, and snaps, with you in the way. Then you might get to be on News at 11 in a way you never expected)

Where Mr. Tourist and I differ is in our response to the knowledge that outside consequences are few and unevenly applied. Mr. Tourist and his spiritual children respond by running rampant. My goal is to keep right on offering "please" and "thank you" the way I was taught. It's my own version of random acts of kindness. And it can make a difference, even if only in that it shocks the bejesus out of somebody thoroughly conditioned to the boorishness that has become almost a national norm.

Finding Civility Again

So what is "civility"?

Ask, and you will receive a laundry list: courtesy, respectability, self-control, regard for others, willingness to follow socially approved rules even if you'd like to do otherwise. It can also mean treating an antagonist with respect, without surrendering your position. Boy is this tough when everyone wants to be right! The opposite, of course, incivility, is discourteous behavior, rudeness, using profanity loudly in public places, flipping the finger to a driver who has offended you, heaping contempt on an antagonist. The funny thing is, it's so easy for everyone to define what it means to be civil, but it seems to be impossible to achieve.

Civility doesn't start with imposition of some outside code, or substitution of laws to govern public behavior for the old religious monoliths, not in my opinion. Laws in and of themselves will not dissuade people from inappropriate and offensive behavior. Civility starts with a personal decision not to play by the ugly rules, not to escalate. I call it "picking your battles," but it really translates into putting things into perspective. How important are the battles that you have chosen to fight today? Civility starts with you and me following our own ethical code in the face of the pressures of the day.

Civility also means having consideration for others. Some of the examples that come to mind are: not cutting other people off in traffic, not racing for a parking spot, holding the door for others as you enter a store or office building, and not letting your children run screaming around a bookstore like wild animals. Those are just off the top of my head. But what they all have in common ties in to another facet of civility and that is being aware of how your behavior affects those around you. It means saying you're sorry and being accountable when you mess up or when your behavior isn't exactly ideal. Our mothers always told us that it took a bigger person to admit they were wrong and I think it still holds true today.

Oh, I know the intellectual arguments against civility. They might sound persuasive on their face. Many of them were first put forward in the tumultuous 1960s, which is the period many cite as the real beginning of all this "self-expression" at the expense of social peace. How about "invigorated liberalism?" In an article in *American Prospect Journal*, a gentleman by the name of Randall Kennedy proposed that such vigorous liberalism required "an insistence upon grappling with the substance of controversies; and a willingness to fight loudly, openly, militantly, even rudely for policies and values…"

He goes on to suggest that such wide-open brouhahas are more conducive to "social flourishing" than a return to some basic courtesies.

I am all for open and free-wheeling debate on the issues which beset us. I nourish a modest hope that my book will contribute to that debate. I agree with Mr. Kennedy that many of our debates today focus on issues that are wildly divisive, with extremists on both sides taking and holding the limelight at all costs. I don't agree that extremism and loud rudeness is the best or only way to address these difficult issues.

A political strategist for President Clinton's 1992 campaign was quoted in newspapers at the time as saying while harshness in political dialogue has been a feature of American life, it has worsened. That policy differences move quickly to personal attacks. *The New York Times* reported in late 1999 that incivility in civic life is becoming more common and more hostile, and described behavior among city councils, county assemblies and even school boards as "boorish, menacing, even violent." Interesting behavior from those people in our society who are supposed to be "leaders."

Also late in the last days of the twentieth century, *U.S. News & World Report* cited a poll about general everyday civility. Twenty-five percent of respondents said Americans are "not very civil" and 59 percent said "somewhat."

But when asked how they treated others, the same group rated themselves as 67 percent very civil and 32 percent somewhat civil.

Was lack of civility a serious problem? The report indicated 47 percent thought it was very serious and 41 percent thought it was somewhat serious.

What's going on here to achieve results like that? To paraphrase the old Quaker saying: is all the world incivil save for me and thee, and frankly sometimes I have my doubts about thee? Are we (you and I) in denial about how our own behavior affects others, but able to see a bit more clearly how theirs affects us? Instead of figuring it's someone else's fault, how about rethinking how you interact with people? Look at your behavior clearly. Could you improve?

I bet I can. I'm trying to do it. I do not want to wake up one day and find out I'm really just Mr. Tourist by another name, plucking unthinkingly at one of the threads that might just unravel this great nation of ours into completely alienated, warring factions.

Serious Social Problems

Much has been written on the decline of civility, and much more on social etiquette, which some call the world's oldest virtue. Even friends feel compelled to tell you that you look like hell or have gained too much weight or too often espouse stupid opinions (usually ones they don't agree with). Even those who, like me, decry the decline of good manners seem to think said manners can be set aside until all the "more serious" social problems have been dealt with.

Back to the homily I mentioned. Would it be that far of a stretch to suppose that the decline of manners and civility is the root cause of most of those other serious social problems?

Before the twentieth century, propriety and good manners were considered on a par with morality. Lately, they seem to be regarded as frippery, not worth the effort. Murder is immoral; humiliation of a person is unmannerly. I think there is ample evidence to conclude that unmannerliness can lead to all sorts of immorality, up to and including homicide.

That Golden Rule I spoke of earlier was an early human attempt, in whatever culture and by whatever name, to encourage empathy. To teach us to think of others as ourselves. The prevailing view today seems to run counter to that, creating an attitude that the wishes of others do not matter. Civility in all its forms was meant to promote social harmony by reducing or controlling such attitudes and to remind us that we aren't the only ones on the planet.

Civility in our daily discourse is the exercise of empathy. It's a good first step toward fostering a public morality, and a buffer zone in that morality's absence. Incivility leads to displays of aggressive behavior—vocal or otherwise—similar to a great ape's pounding on its puffed up chest. And such chest-pounding can lead to violence, once the pounder is worked up enough. Vocal or physical violence, the pattern seems to be the same: loss of civility, rise of aggressive behavior, attack.

As you move out into your world tomorrow, I ask you to consider the merits that a return to simple courtesy across this nation could bring to us. Please?

And thank you.

CHAPTER 2

Dumbing Down

EVER BEEN IN A MCDONALD'S RESTAURANT WHEN THE "SMART" CASH REG-
ISTERS GO DOWN? You know, those clever machines with the pictures of
bags of French fries and the like, so the servers don't have to remember
prices or key in an inventory code? Buy $5.47 worth of food and watch
the poor kid behind the counter sweat bullets counting out the change
for a ten-dollar-bill. You'll probably join the growing multitude of
Americans who seem to wonder, just what are they teaching in these
schools of ours?

Those machines are just one example of how, in our quest for "faster,
easier, cheaper," we are giving in to our inclination to simple slide by
without any real effort. This affects not just our physical bodies, but
our minds as well, dulling our reflexes, slowing our natural inclination
to learn. We're already dealing with a television culture that encour-
ages laziness in ourselves and our children and we battle daily over the
desire to "see the movie" and not "read the book." Doesn't something as
small as not having to count back change make a sad comment on the
state of education in this country today? Is this what we want our future to look like?

And the dumbing down of America seems to cut across all ethnic
and financial boundaries. During the Gulf War, there were sizable anti-
war protests around federal buildings in some cities across the nation,
like a reprise of the Vietnam protest days. A high-school history
teacher in one of those cities, whose civil-servant spouse was jostled

rudely by the demonstrators, called the governor's office. She complained that the city's mayor was not permitting the police to sweep demonstrators off the sidewalks around the federal building. She demanded, and this is no joke sadly, that the governor "fire the mayor" and take over!

This, mind you, from a teacher charged with shaping the thoughts of hundreds of our young people across her career! You'd expect a history teacher to have a basic understanding of how political subdivisions operate within our nation. Wouldn't you?

I certainly would!

Now before all you fully qualified and terribly frustrated teachers across the nation take pen in hand (or tar and feathers), I know one or two anecdotes don't condemn a profession. The issues confronting the educational institutions of our nation are many and thorny. Some might even say intractable.

The dumbing down of education is, unfortunately, an accurate reflection of the general dumbing down of America. There are things that schools are ill equipped to do for a child who comes to school unprepared to learn. The reasons for that unpreparedness create a demographic profile of this land of ours. Here are a few:

- children whose parents are hardly more than children themselves, and barely literate;

- latchkey children from two-income homes where the parents are hard put to find any time to spend with their offspring, let alone "quality time" which might stimulate brain cells;

- children from the inner-city battle zones, whose role models are the corner crack dealer or foul-mouthed entertainment celebrities.

Are We Spending Enough?

When faced with this set of demographics, what have we chosen to do? Throw dollars, dollars and more dollars at it. An estimated $350 billion is spent in this nation annually on primary and secondary schools, administered by a crazy quilt of local school boards. Almost everyone you talk to will pay lip service to the importance of education and we're a nation that doesn't take any voting day very seriously anyway, but school-board elections consistently record the lightest turnout. School bond issues almost routinely get voted down across this fair land.

School administration is so stifled by red tape it can hardly function. Though the federal government only weighs in with roughly seven percent of that vast sum cited above, it does attempt to mandate special programs for the underprivileged and the paperwork required of local school boards for that purpose is overwhelming.

Meanwhile, kids continue to drop out, fail, and wind up in dead-end jobs or in jail. Employers are hard pressed to find employees with basic skills. I recall a Chicago bank that had to create its own in-house school to teach basic writing and math skills to potential employees. It wasn't the first and it won't be the last company to have to go this route.

And guess who pays? We do. Twice. In my example, property taxes paid for the public education that did not "take" and the customers of that bank paid with higher fees for services. I hope the bank's second education "took" because I'd hate to think of paying for it a third time.

Why Doesn't Public Education Work Better?

Beneath all the rhetoric on education, all the billions thrown at the problem and all the struggles of thousands of dedicated educators, I think that is the central burning question: why doesn't public education work better?

The answer is simple: we have lost our way. We no longer have a clear, unified vision of exactly what we want our children to learn. We are floundering, because we have either forgotten who we, as a culture are—or if we haven't forgotten, we want to apologize for it—or we're so interested in our individual gains, we adopt a "can't see the forest for the trees" mentality. As long as the weather's good on this side of the block, we can ignore what it means to be "we the people."

And just who are we? We are the United States of America that's who. One of the noblest experiments of the human mind, the brainchild of an assembly of minds (our Founding Fathers) the like of which this world has seldom seen. I'm not here to argue that it was fair that Europeans imposed their will on the first Americans, or that everything American is perfect and iconic and beyond reproach. But the American dream is that here, in this marvelous land, anyone can invent, or reinvent, themselves, nearer to their heart's desire. And a tenet of that creed is that one of the most powerful tools for doing so is education.

Right now, today, our culture is full of stories of refugee kids who arrive on these shores without a smidgen of English and wind up valedictorian of their high school class, and ten years later, own their own business or have risen to the top of whatever field they selected. In common with earlier waves of immigrants, they purchased the American dream of education as the great equalizer, and made it work.

At the other end of the spectrum are our native-born kids, with this grand nation as their birthright. They come to school from teen parents, from the welfare rolls, from broken homes, or worse. They grow to school age in dismal projects or ghettos that would make Dickens' London look like a vacation resort, and they are surrounded by crack dealers and pimps. They have little or no sense of family, no sense of personal safety, or of self-worth. The miracle is that any of these kids can turn their minds to the abstractions of learning and make it through at all, seems to me. Of course even in the seamiest neighborhoods there still exist the hard-working single mothers or poverty-stricken parents, working one or more dead-end jobs to make enough money to put their kids through school, and to provide a fragile bubble of normalcy to nourish the developing minds in their care.

In the big middle lie the millions of two-income households where parents struggle and often fail to provide all the goodies our consumer society dictates as necessity. Cars, wide-screen TVs, expensive sneakers, designer jeans. And the TV becomes the babysitter for latchkey kids, who form their attitudes from an unmonitored and steady drum roll of TV violence, sex—and commercials for more and better goodies. Worse, this focus so totally dominates that the most important tenets—discipline, a work ethic, manners, respect for others—have fallen by the wayside, fallen victim to the (preferably easy) stampede for the good stuff. It doesn't matter how we get it as long as we get it.

The Dumbing Down

When did this slide into the dumbing down of America begin? I think it began with the wholesale rebellion of youth in reaction to the

Vietnam War. Without commenting on the righteousness (or lack there-of) of antiwar sentiment, I note that the movement culminated in the spirit of "do your own thing" without regard to anyone else. The idea spread like wildfire—or like the plague—and personal responsibility became laughable.

When I nominate the 1960s for the beginning of the decline, I'm not alone. In her excellent book, *When the Bough Breaks*, Sylvia Ann Hewlitt documents that during the 1950s, TV networks still broadcast 27 hours a week of "squeaky clean" family programming such as the "Mickey Mouse Club" and "Watch Mr. Wizard." Evening prime time was devoted to shows like "Ozzie and Harriet" and "Father Knows Best," which reflected the cultural norms of the majority of American households then.

Before the advocates of ethnocentrism and alternate lifestyles rise up, I would like to point out that those without these cultural norms also aspired to them. One of the most heartbreaking things I've ever heard is the story of a young boy who finally reported his sexually abusive parent to school authorities. During counseling he was asked how he developed the courage to do so. He said that after watching many episodes of "Leave it to Beaver," it finally dawned on him that what was cloaked in secrecy within his shattered household was not the way things were supposed to be.

Heartbreaking as it is, this vignette speaks to me of something our culture began to lose in the 1960s, with the advent of "The Untouch-ables," "Route 66" and other similar TV shows. These were so violent that they prompted the U.S. Senate to set up a subcommittee on Juve-nile Delinquency to study the link between TV violence and burgeon-ing violence among our young.

The violent shows were popular though. The networks accelerated their programming. The studies and surveys kept rolling in, all pointing to links between viewing television violence and aggressive social be-havior in juveniles. The Federal Communications Commission (FCC) finally was spurred to action in the 1970s, and by the end of that decade had proposed rulemaking to require at least 7 1/2 hours of age-appropriate children's programs per week.

Reagan and the FCC

Then came the Reagan years, and virtual worship of the marketplace. The FCC rulemaking never happened. Mark Fowler, Reagan's FCC chair, was quoted as saying if five million children wanted to watch Oprah instead of do their homework they had an absolute right to do so. Millions of kids are exercising that right in front of the boob tube as I type these words, and on fare that is far less appealing than Oprah.

Then there are the commercials.

Hewlitt reported in her book that by the time a young person reaches high school graduation age, he or she will have been exposed to 1500 hours of TV commercials, or the equivalent of a full work year! The number has probably risen since she published, thanks to the proliferation of channels.

Every commercial is designed to make the viewer "want, want, want," with no mention of how to go about earning the wherewithal to "get." So we see the spectacle of school children beating or killing each other for a pair of expensive sneakers or warmup jacket.

It's almost a stone-age reaction among our youth.

"Nike good. Want Nike. You got Nike. Me TAKE Nike."

Why does it work this way? Because children must be *taught* standards of behavior and conduct, and yes, even good old-fashioned manners. They don't come into the world predisposed to be gentle and kind! Absent strong familial guidance and exposed to the constant barrage of "me-ism," any moral compass simply is missing. Ever notice how confused these young hooligans look in their jail coveralls as they are paraded after the latest atrocity? They still don't get why it's any big deal!

Our Nation's Principles

Which leads me back to the principles of our Founding Fathers. This nation was founded upon the belief that all are entitled to life, liberty and the pursuit of happiness. But somehow this consumer-age, market-driven society of ours seems to have deleted "pursuit of" in favor of a sense of "entitlement to" happiness.

Want shoes, take shoes. Me, me, me—it's always all about me.

Against the constant din of the unbridled marketplace, what chance do our schools stand of producing good citizens? Is it even their job to do so?

In the best of all possible worlds, parents would do more of this. In the real world, schools are often our last bastion against a generation of barbarians. And in any event, elementary and secondary education should perform the principle function of instilling cultural literacy in its charges, as well as the good old solid reading, writing and 'rithmetic.

What do I mean by cultural literacy?

I mean teaching our kids who we, as Americans, are supposed to be, and who we are as citizens. The tenets of a good citizen, to me, are straightforward. One would be the willingness to serve on a jury. Another is the interest in the long-term future of the country; that entails not just voting but voting with awareness. Try having respect for the next generation and not simply living for yourself for today. I also think fundamental to everyday good citizenship is for everyone to learn how there came to be a United States of America and what it replaced in the world in terms of monarchies and empires and such. Why our system of governance is set up so carefully. Why the checks and balances of the separation of powers between judicial, executive and legislative were so carefully apportioned by our founders, and are worth preserving.

This would provide a solid foundation for explaining how we became the Great Melting Pot of the world, from the Pilgrims to the Irish of the Potato Famine to the contemporary Asians. America is where the downtrodden or the unlucky of the Old World came to reinvent themselves, and make a better place for their progeny. Their progeny need to learn an appreciation of all the blood, sweat and tears it took to make the world safe for Sony Walkmans. As Americans we have our own lingo, our own worldview, our own destiny.

America Rules

We are the dominant culture of the age. I say that without apology. Imperial China may have held that role in ancient times, or Rome in the Mediterranean, but right now, it's us. Do you know of any other country where people will stow away like dried goods in virtually airless containers for danger-laden sea voyages, paying thousands of dollars for the privilege, just to be smuggled in as illegal aliens? America remains a lodestone of hope on a planet teeming with troubled masses, and our own children, largely blind to its promise, somehow fail to grasp how special their birthright is. No wonder they seem like a lost generation.

We either incorporate the necessary values while we can, in school, or we spawn a generation of barbarians! Somebody has to civilize these urchins.

Along with the civilizing must be taught fundamental skills. A philosophical understanding of democracy won't help much if the voter can't read the ballot. School systems across the nation struggle to find the best model to produce the most reliable results in basic skills. Teaching is not easy work in the best circumstances, and given the strikes already against so many of our children before teachers get to them, even getting the three Rs right is not a simple task. Everything I have read indicates that it is very difficult to find a replicable model for teaching that will deliver consistently. In my reading, though, one thing stands out clearly: where there is a passionate teacher to motivate students, good things happen. Almost everyone is familiar with "Stand and Deliver," the story of Jaime Escalante and how he inspired the unlikeliest students to amazing scholastic successes, and much enhanced self-esteem along the way. Reflecting on that, I wish there were some way to clone such excellent human beings by the hundreds, and put them in all our classrooms.

The Merit of Merit Pay

More practically speaking, we need to identify the excellent teachers, agree upon what makes them excellent, and reward that excellence. We must recruit the best and brightest, and reward them sufficiently to stay in teaching. While I am very big on the United States, and very proud of our culture overall, other industrialized nations do a lot better job at this. Teachers get more respect and more pay. In this country, reward usually is understood to mean higher pay, which translates into higher taxes, and heels get dug in. Reluctant admission that remuneration needs to be improved is linked to a demand for some standard to ensure the taxpayers are getting what they pay for. "Merit pay" is mentioned. But let the word "merit" enter the conversations here, and boy does the fur fly! One man's merit is another man's pork barrel.

Before we can ever approach a system that seeks out and rewards excellence in teaching—and thereby gives our children the best shot at learning—we will have to establish iron-clad standards for what excellence is. Test score results? Definitely. Something against which performance can be measured and agreed upon. If we can get to that, we can begin to reward those teachers who bring excellence to the learning experience. Attract more and better individuals to the profession. And see the slow shift over years, as inspired students begin to move through the system. It's not a quick fix, but the effect of such teaching lasts.

I should point out, however, that what I'm suggesting here is quite literally an investment in our future as a nation. Even should we achieve such agreed-upon standards, however, we're still not out of the woods entirely. One of the biggest stumbling blocks will remain our egalitarian view of education. The old American tradition that a comprehensive education is good for everyone, or a rising tide lifts all boats, simply is not subscribed to elsewhere.

How Should We Educate Our Young?

Other industrialized nations test their children early for academic excellence, and the tests have teeth in them. Children who don't make the cut are diverted into less challenging curricula or into vocational and other forms of training. From England to Japan, very young children whose test scores do not reflect an affinity for higher learning don't get a second chance. Thus, the best teachers are presented the best, most motivated students.

I'm not suggesting that is the finest system, though it certainly does show measurable academic results. After all, what of the poor late bloomer? Such a lack of opportunity, even as a concept, sets uneasily with Americans. But I would submit that the opposite extreme—trying to educate all alike to a high degree—is attempting the impossible.

It seems to me a middle road, where students' affinities come into play, might offer fertile ground. There are many people who prefer working with their hands to working with equations. In this of all countries, there should be no stigma attached to that. Students who want a career in car repair or plumbing should be granted the same excellent teachers as those who want academic achievement. No industrialized society is going to be worth a damn unless it has plumbers who are just as good as its philosophers.

I think it's a sad irony in our determinedly egalitarian society that a "blue collar" in the United States carries such a stigma. We continue to pay lip service to universal education, but the execution falls far short, and leaves thousands of unhappy, sometimes unemployable people in its wake. That's an awful human toll to pay for the concept that everyone should be academically adept.

It's time to face up to this problem squarely, deal with societal expectations and restore dignity to hands-on toil. We need to redesign our schools to channel those minds which thirst for it toward higher education, and provide an avenue for an employable, happy life to those that don't. Otherwise we wind up with the spectacle so common back in the 1980s, of people with advanced physics degrees managing a chain hamburger joint. A lot of those somewhat-bitter young people might well ask, what was the point of all the education if this is all it's good for?

Now there are indeed those who love knowledge for its own sake, and who would happily pursue their studies while waiting tables or repairing computers. More power to them. But I suspect an awful lot of young people would rather have opportunities to learn how to do something useful, a skill or a trade, something to give them economic autonomy. Why compel them to wait until they graduate from high school and have to go get that experience on their own?

Let's Get Practical

While I'm on the subject of practical learning, I think school is the place for young people to be taught the basics of living in this complex society of ours.

I call this the literacy of day-to-day living.

Surely we can find a semester or two to teach the basics: managing a checking account; how to handle consumer credit; what to do at income tax time; what to know about health and other forms of insurance; and last but not least, how to evaluate the prospects of marriage and parenthood. Boys and girls are going to get together, and unless they know to be careful, they're going to have children; why not give them solid information about the mechanics of family and parenting beyond "sex ed"? A marriage is an institution, and needs a lot of work; having children is a major responsibility. At some point these young people need to be exposed to the cumulative knowledge of society, or they will be doomed to repeat the cycles their own parents did— which led to much of this mess to start with.

Am I asking too much of our beleaguered schools? I don't think so.

For all the vastness of our land, and the diversity of our backgrounds, contemporary parents, when asked, show a considerable unity across race, class, and gender as to what is needed for our children. Our leaders need to tap this unity and stop using education as a political football. Whether professional or blue-collar, suburbanites or inner-city dwellers, parents want practical education for their offspring. Education that shows measurable results. In this regard, perhaps surprisingly, many of us are on the same page. Multi-culturalism and ethnocentric studies and all the rest of the new-age stuff about which such hyperbole has been thrown around is largely viewed as frippery or "feel good" stuff, right across the board. I couldn't agree more.

Parental Time Famine

Parents from all walks of life seem united in a concern for practical issues. From the working poor to the professionals, their main concern is time crunch. I've seen the term "parental time famine" used. And the sound-bite solution most often used to counter that concern is "quality time." Parents struggling to make ends meet, whether in the inner city or burdened with an enormous suburban mortgage and two (or more) car payments, wonder why the job of raising their offspring is such a lonely and thankless struggle. Don't government and business have a vital interest in the kinds of citizens our children will become? You bet they do!

Our schools then must be the focal civilizing influence. I'm leaning more and more toward the kind of institution that requires school uniforms—an outward and visible sign that the school day is serious business. Fancy clothing is a distraction, and only serves to underline the differences between haves and have nots. School should not be a place to be ashamed of the amount of wear on your jeans, or vain about your gaudy sneakers. Uniforms send a strong signal to the less-well-off that here in school at least, there is a level playing field. To the well-to-do, it sends another signal: that while you are here, you will focus on the task of learning. You have the rest of your life to adopt the superficial values of your acquisitive parents.

The contemporary violence, kids hurting or killing kids for their fancy clothing, is horrifying. But clothing disparity has long played a role in the "Lord of the Flies" hierarchical interaction of the undisciplined young. Every generation has its "must-have" attire, driven by a marketplace zeroed in on making big bucks out of a need to "fit in." From white bucks and Gant shirts with locker loops to shiny warm-up jackets and space-age sneakers, the underlying need to be "with it" or "cool" drives the sales.

In my own school days—way back in the middle of the late century—we city kids could spot the "shit-kickers" a mile away. By which we meant rural farm kids, some of who had neatly patched holes in their worn jeans. Did we care that those knees probably had been worn out in back-breaking toil beside their parents on a family farm, in order to feed the community? We did not. We just knew they were different from us, odd, and therefore fair game. Maybe violence then was restricted to taunts and an occasional knuckle sandwich—but that was because most of us still lived in two-parent households, and because our communities and our teachers and principals didn't take much guff from any of us.

Fast forward to today. It's not that far a stretch, given today's daily regimen of violence in the media and entertainment industries, to the horror of a Columbine High School massacre. What the assailants did was awful and unforgivable—but it is what can happen when children are marginalized and stigmatized by the stylish cliques. It was Blackboard Jungle with repeating weapons instead of switchblades. Hundreds of children quietly suffer the indignities and bear psychic scars all their lives from their school days. The ones who react violently grab the headlines.

School Administration's Duty

In addition to education, I believe a significant duty of our school administrators and teachers today is to protect the pariah, instill good citizenship in all their wayward charges, and teach compassion and empathy for each other. We can lament all we want that these are values that should have been inculcated in the home—but clearly they have not been, for myriad reasons. To continue to lament the breakdown of family values is like sitting on the side of the road whining because you have a flat tire. The tire doesn't get fixed. Our cultural vehicle is in danger of having four flats at once. It's time to jack it up and start putting on some fresh tread!

So that's my prescription for schools. Find a way to reinstill cultural literacy in our young, a sense of who we are as a nation and as a people; find a way to encourage and support excellent teachers who can inspire their charges to excellence in their academic pursuits—or in their vocational training—and teach some basic skills for living in this complex society of ours. And I believe it all can be accomplished, one school district at a time.

What it needs is for you the citizen of these United States, whether your children are long grown and gone or not, to care enough about our heritage to get involved at that local district level. Take ownership of the problem, and address it. Americans have shown over and over that they can perform miracles when they put their minds and hearts and shoulders to it. And given the state of our educational edifice today, a miracle may be just about what the doctor ordered!

CHAPTER 3

"Victimless Crime"

WHAT EXACTLY IS A "VICTIMLESS" CRIME? This term is usually applied to a "crime" you commit against yourself. Three major categories of activity—while often criminalized and demonized by society—do not really fit a common sense definition of crime, in terms of having a victim against whom the perpetrator acts. In using illegal drugs, in consorting with prostitutes, or in throwing your money away on games of chance, the principal victim of your perpetration is yourself.

Yes, there are secondary victims as well. The family of the drunken layabout is not provided for, in the classic example put forward by the temperance movement which led to nationwide Prohibition. And oh yes, liquor is definitely a drug; it is just handled differently than other drugs. Regulated instead of banned.

So let's take a look at these three categories that society has tried with varying degrees of success—or failure—to ban, to regulate, to control.

The Futile War On Narcotics

Technically, smoking two packs of cigarettes a day isn't a crime, because cigarettes aren't illegal (yet!) but few would argue that it is an abuse of your body. In this context, recreational drug use is a victimless crime. Purportedly, you're only hurting yourself.

Now before you squawk about all the brutality associated with drugs that we read and hear about in the media, let me point out that most of that falls into three categories:

America in Crisis

1) **Distribution disputes.** Organized crime groups which distribute illegal substances have been battling over turf since Thompson submachine guns were adapted from World War One by bootleggers and nicknamed "Chicago typewriters." Much of the shooting and blowing up and "Colombian neckties" of today are hoodlums killing hoodlums. If recreational drug distribution were as legal as liquor distribution today, perhaps these killings would stop.

2) **Overdoses.** The emergency rooms of our nation are the site of countless tragic deaths from drug users, but closer examination shows that many of these deaths are associated with adulterated product, unknown dosages and the like. Results of the substance itself being illegally obtained, without any regard to purity or strength. Were recreational drugs regulated like meat and poultry and antibiotics, most of this mortality might also stop.

3) **Robberies, muggings and killings** of innocent third parties by strung-out junkies seeking to finance their next fix. Here, the economics of illegal distribution are at fault. Demand is high, the risks of distribution great, and the distributors charge what the market will bear.

Street costs have very little to do with the actual cost of producing a pure product. Again, a legal distribution system, with all the uncertainties removed, would drop the costs well within a range where habitual users could afford a maintenance level of their addiction.

So strip away all the bloody horror of the turf wars, the ODs and the crazed addicts, and we are left with the core issue: is it our business as a society to coerce all of our members away from this particular self-destructive habit, when tens of thousands of our citizens are determined to partake? Is it in our best interest as a free nation to even try?

I have to say, our history says no.

I'm talking about the failed effort to dry this nation up, one example of how the country has tried to do battle with addiction that takes place on an individual level.

Liquor had been a staple of American existence since the colonial period. The colonial and frontier view of liquor use was that it was a valued social custom, it made harsh life a little easier to bear, and excessive use or abuse was an individual character flaw. The solution: clap the drunk in stocks or throw him in the drunk tank.

But as the nation marched to the Pacific and the frontier began to close, a temperance movement took solid root across the land. The term "Demon Rum" came into play; the so-called "Drys" believed liquor was an addicting poison of no redeeming social value, and proper policy was to remove it from the reach of all. To say that was a hard sell to a nation with more than its share of two-fisted drinkers is an understatement, but never underestimate the tenacity of zealots. Twenty years after our frontier was officially declared closed, they had the votes, and America went "dry."

It's been over eighty years since the last necessary state ratified the Eighteenth Amendment to the Constitution of the United States, and the era known variously as "Prohibition" or "The Noble Experiment" came into full force and effect.

It still needed an Act of Congress to authorize the Administration to enforce it, and an ultra-religious congressman from Minnesota, Andrew J. Volstead, soon supplied that Act. Bolstered by the triumphant evangelicals who had barnstormed the Eighteenth Amendment to success, Volstead's Act went even further: it defined "intoxicating liquors" to include any beverage with more than one half of one percent alcohol. Not even President Wilson's veto could stop the anti-drinking tide.

"They can never repeal it," Volstead exulted.

But repeal it they did, after a long and bloody struggle that gave us a lasting legacy of organized crime and official corruption.

If Prohibition taught us anything, it should have been that in a free nation, where there is an overwhelming public acceptance of a particular activity, it is fruitless to try to prohibit that activity. The more Draconian the measures employed in the attempt to stop the activity, the more creative become the efforts to circumvent those measures. At the same time, respect for the law and its enforcers wanes quickly. You can take prohibition only so far in a free society.

Which brings us back to the so-called war on drugs.

We have reached the point where government functionaries can seize homes, personal property, bank accounts—any and all of an individual's possessions—as part of a drug investigation. As far as the marital community goes, community property be damned. If the husband is a suspect, the wife's share of the home is lost too. The entire scheme of confiscatory authority smacks strongly of King George and his Redcoats—but to speak against it can mean being labelled as soft on drugs.

The anti-drug rhetoric these days remains as heated and as pervasive as did the tracts of the Anti-Saloon League and the Temperance Movement through all the years leading up to and during Prohibition. In fact, history shows that some of the same evangelicals who crusaded so fiercely against Demon Rum (and teaching Darwin's theories in our schools) rallied in the 1930s behind the nation's first-ever "drug czar," Harry Anslinger. Anslinger, a humorless Fed in the mold of J. Edgar Hoover (whom some believed Anslinger envied his press clippings) had a particular hatred for marijuana.

As Prohibition died its largely unlamented death, it left a strange legacy. Bootleggers with fleets of trucks and no whiskey to haul turned to regular commerce, bringing with them all their underworld competitive "business" techniques. On the government side, agents with years to go until retirement shifted neatly from alcohol to drugs as a raison d'etre. A whole new fanfare of propaganda rolled across the land, gaining in intensity. Anslinger reportedly attempted to fuel much of this by concentrating his efforts on gathering evidence for allegations of drug use by famous musicians from Jimmy Dorsey to Duke Ellington, with a dream of arresting them all on the same night—the raid to end all raids. He'd show that Hoover clown! But cooler heads prevailed, and the mega raid never occurred.

Still, the stage for the abortive war on drugs was set.

Ever since, the government has tried successively elaborate methods of interdicting drug traffic, and increasingly harsher laws. Current estimates place the annual cost of the drug war at an estimated $75 billion (that's "billion" with a "b") of taxpayers' money—that's your and my hard earned dollars. As the famous Senator Everett Dirksen was fond of saying, a billion here and a billion there and pretty soon you're talking about real money.

An estimated half of the Americans behind bars today are there because of drug-related crimes, ranging upwards from possession of relatively small amounts of a controlled substance.

Half the trial days of all our criminal courts are consumed in drug cases, according to these same estimates. It's not unheard of for burglars and rapists to be set free early or on parole in order to open jail bunks for narcotics "mules," the worker ants who attempt to smuggle drugs into this country.

President Clinton grabbed big headlines with his proposal to fund an additional 100,000 policemen several years back. But if an administrative decision to redirect existing police forces away from the attempt to curtail drug commerce were made, an additional 400,000 cops would become available for duty! At no extra cost!

Homeowners who find their abode ransacked and are told to call the insurance company, told that there's too much of a backlog for a robbery investigation, might well ponder this idea of 400,000 extra cops for a moment.

Let's just consider the practical ramifications of legalization of drugs. For the sake of argument, say we turn control of drug sales over to states, and they administer them through state stores, much as some states control liquor sales. The pricing reflects actual cost of manufacture and shipping and stocking, with a reasonable markup to fund, say, education or health care. No advertising allowed. Identification required to purchase.

To return to the Prohibition model briefly, when Prohibition was lifted, the third social theory of alcohol abuse took concrete form: addiction is a disease, and proper policy is treatment of the addict. Less than a decade elapsed between Repeal and the rise nationwide of Alcoholics Anonymous. Intense study into alcohol addiction is an on-going effort.

But Repeal did not result in a nation awash with sodden drunks.

Experts in chemical dependency are on record as saying repeal of the drug laws would not result in a nation of zombies either. Plenty of citizens today—millions—indulge in illegal drugs when they feel like it, and avoid them when they don't.

Zombies we will always have with us, until the addiction gene is tracked down somewhere along that double helix of DNA, and a method devised to snip it out. There will always be a percentage of people who are incorrigibly unproductive, who prefer their opium pipe or jug of cheap wine to a real life.

I sometimes think a litmus test of a free society may be how well we tolerate that irreducible minimum of such incorrigibles. Vagrants, drifters, the rootless and the hopeless. I don't much like to think I am laboring to support such people with my tax dollars, but that's really a whole different issue than the issue of self-victimization through use of drugs.

I know all of this sounds almost subversive in light of the government-sanctioned propaganda war against drug use. But remember: it is a propaganda war. Just as Demon Rum was the tract equivalent of a sound bite, and Reefer Madness was a fabrication of a government-coerced Hollywood, the latest and most terrifying bogey man appears to be Crack. Urban legends about the terrifying aspects of a Crack user abound. But neuroscientists—the people who study the human brain and nervous system—don't subscribe to them. Crack, they explain, is simply cocaine stirred together with baking soda and water, and boiled. This technique permits cocaine to be smoked, and the smoke absorbed by the lungs gets to the brain faster, producing a quicker high. But the specific effect on the brain is identical to cocaine's, the active ingredient—no one has suggested baking soda creates Frankenstein monsters!

It is probable that Crack's lethal reputation stems, once more, from the economics of illegal distribution. "Stepping on" cocaine to form Crack makes for a less expensive product, one within the reach of the inner-city poor, the disenfranchised, the hopeless. For a brief respite, things don't seem so awful—and then the effect wears off, and there are the same bombed-out tenements and junk strewn streets. The tendency is to want more, to escape again—and of course the money runs out, since there wasn't much to start with. No job, no means to support the habit—violence is the almost preordained result.

Given legal distribution channels, it has been argued that pure cocaine would be available to the consumer for prices rivaling Crack now. According to the scientists, the pure stuff provides a more lasting effect, and given freedom of choice, almost anyone would opt for that. So we're back to where I began this chapter—most of the mayhem and bloodshed associated with the war on drugs seems to be a result of their illegality, not of their intrinsic chemical properties.

The United States started out to be a free nation, where its citizens enjoyed the rights to life, liberty and the pursuit of happiness. If millions of our fellow citizens prefer to pursue their happiness through the ingestion or inhalation of various substances, and have demonstrated their determination to do so against increasingly frightening exercise of the police power of the state, isn't it time to rethink the whole issue? Really rethink it?

Is use of drugs actually a crime? Against whom? If it is against some overblown sense of propriety—that others simply shouldn't do stuff like that—is pursuing this war to its bitter end really worth a Prohibition-like legacy of disrespect for all law and government? Is it worth dividing our nation violently into those who don't dare, never would think of it—and those who flout attempts to dissuade them? Is it worth the continued carnage wrought by the illegal trade?

What do you think? What do you really think?

The Oldest Profession

Prostitution is a subject heavily charged with emotion. Societies throughout history have dealt with it in varying ways, from formally incorporating it into the social fabric to attempting to eradicate it altogether.

The latter approach has never worked.

What it has accomplished, where employed, is to create an underworld enterprise of "fancy" houses or pimps, sleazy entrepreneurs who prey off the sexual labor of their charges. I suppose there may have been madams with hearts of gold, as appear in some literature. I'm harder pressed to believe there ever was a pimp with a heart at all. Under the ground rules of illegal prostitution, unfortunately, many of the practitioners are on a par with slaves. Wholly owned chattel.

If we strip aside the odious superstructure which accompanies the essential act of prostitution, and look at the basic transaction, what do we have?

A woman—or a man—who exchanges the sexual use of her or his body for financial recompense. If an individual should choose this form of enterprise willingly, without coercion or forced addiction to narcotics, what is the essential difference between that and manual labor such as digging ditches or flipping hamburgers?

This is a topic that makes many people queasy. Aside from the moral implications are the health implications: sexually transmitted diseases have always been a threat, and now more so than ever.

The health issues, though, could be addressed through regulation, not prohibition. Men are going to seek prostitutes, regardless of the laws. The market is there, and there will always be someone to meet the market demand. Turning a blind eye to its existence, because the law says it is illegal, leaves the enterprise unregulated and unsupervised. Are pimps likely to be intelligent enough, or socially conscious enough, to ensure their girls are healthy? Evidence suggests otherwise. There are always fresh faces to recruit, looking for the "easy" money and the ability to sleep in mornings. No time-clock punching here.

It is my contention you erode support for society and its laws if you attempt to ban or prohibit activities in which a significant proportion of the population are determined to indulge. Disobedience of unenforceable laws sets the tone for more disobedience, and disrespect for the law can become widespread.

If a prospective prostitute could freely enter or leave "the life" without pressure from pimps or criminal organizations, was required to undergo regular health checkups, and educated in the use of contraception and prevention of STDs, what arguments could logically remain against such regulation in place of prohibition?

A) **That the practitioner is abusing her/his body?**
Well, it's their body. We don't ban cigarettes, though I know many would like to. (And such a "Nicotine Prohibition" would probably lead to dancing and hand clapping in underworld circles.) If a woman has the right to determine whether or not to carry a fetus to term, does she not have the right to determine how she uses her body in other matters?

B) **That our sense of propriety and right living is outraged?**
If all the government regulation and oversight of prostitution would offend is a somewhat hazy sense of propriety, then perhaps it's time for us to reshape our ideas of propriety. The pre-

sent state of prohibition may square with propriety, but it comes with a horrific toll of violence against sex workers by their "supervisors," of compelled drug addiction, of lethal STDs and wasted lives.

There have been scores of studies done around the world about the incidence of human immunodeficiency virus (HIV) in prostitutes. One source for this information was *www.worldsexguide.org*. Here are a couple of examples from their bibliography:

A medical study attributed to a team named Kopp and Dangl-Erlach, 1986, reportedly found only 0.8 percent of 839 Vienna prostitutes, where prostitution is registered and regulated, to be HIV-positive. Each of the HIV-positive sex workers was either an IV drug user or the sexual partner of an IV drug user. A Netherlands study of 201 non-drug using prostitutes and 213 male clients (Van Haastrecht, 1993) reportedly only three prostitutes and one client infected. All three of the infected prostitutes allegedly were recent migrants from AIDS-endemic countries.

The same web site said it found almost no studies on the incidence of HIV in American prostitutes, and asserted that funding agencies were unwilling to underwrite such work. Propriety again? Ignore it and it will go away?

Scanning results such as those reported above, some have concluded that the incidence of IV drug use is far more of a risk factor for HIV infection than prostitution alone. Even more astonishing, perhaps, they conclude that outside of East Africa, the prevalence of HIV in sex workers is not significantly different than that of the general populations with which these sex workers ply their trade.

An Internet observer whose email address I will keep private for the sake of his sanity comments somewhat laconically:

"If you have no STDs, use a condom, and avoid sex workers with needle marks in the arms, your risk is probably no greater than your risk of getting AIDs from your girlfriend or mistress. If you have a history of STDs, don't use a condom, and use sex workers who are known i.v. drug users...good luck!"

Perhaps one final note here: if sex workers in this country were regulated and protected by the law, they would no longer be the marginalized people they are now, working "the stroll" along dimly lit streets and highways, easy prey for sadistic sex predators.

Interestingly, our civil neighbor to the north, Canada, seems to have developed a discreet form of legalized prostitution which places the decision of whether or not to engage in the work squarely in the hands of the individual. An Internet newsgroup posting describes the following:

Prostitution itself is legal under federal law. Brothels are illegal. It is illegal to live off the income of a prostitute. Prostitutes may not solicit publicly. Only independent practitioners who take calls at home, and then go on an "out-call" are operating within the law.

How discreet. How much safer for the prostitute than the situation here. How…civilized?

Gambling

If humans hadn't been risk-takers, we might never have left the warm African savannahs to populate the world and develop civilization. Ritualized betting appears to have been part of every culture in history, and probably was in pre-history as well.

There are people who will bet on whether the sun will rise.

An old witticism about a compulsive gambler has it that he swore off, told all his friends he would never, ever wager again. His closest friend said who are you trying to kid? You'll never stop.

Will too, the gambler said—I'll give you ten to one odds on it!

Truly compulsive gambling is no joke. It's as addictive and destroying as addictions to liquor or drugs. The National Gambling Impact Study Commission (NGISC) in 1999 estimated that about 2 1/2 million Americans are "pathological" gamblers, and another 3 million fall into the category of problem gamblers, based on criteria established by the American Psychiatric Association.

The commission went on to estimate another 15 million people might be "at risk," while 148 million are low-risk and 29 million have never gambled at all.

This particular victimless crime in recent years has begun to pass from the hands of organized criminal endeavors into state-run lotteries and heavily regulated gaming establishments. The commission looked at community impact of newly opened casinos and found no significant increase in bankruptcy, health, or violent crime rates.

That's not much consolation to the families of the problem gamblers, but they clearly are in the minority. The specific issue of problem gambling is being addressed nationwide by groups ranging from Gamblers Anonymous (modeled on Alcoholics Anonymous) to state gambling commissions which underwrite educational efforts.

My own modest proposal for dealing with the pathological, the problem and the at-risk gambler is rather simple. Establish firm criteria which identify these individuals, assess their incomes, and establish what permissible gambling losses would be. Require them to register with the state gaming authorities. They would go into the state computers, and when they reached their preset limit for the year, they would be cut off from placing bets.

I know this would not stop them from turning to alternative sources to put a bet down, but it would remove an awful lot of temptation.

I suppose a logical extension of this would be to require a computerized gambling license for all who wish to play. Again, we're talking about regulation, not prohibition. The database would ensure that winnings were taxed properly, too. If you want to gamble, you shove your smart card through the magnetic strip in the lottery machine or at the cashier's window in the casino or at the track.

As the NGISC report states, legal gambling activities "become part of the routine processes of government."

Gambling it seems is joining liquor in that regard.

Perhaps one day, so will recreational drug use and prostitution.

CHAPTER 4

Selfishness

NO EVALUATION OF WHAT'S AMISS IN AMERICA TODAY WOULD BE COMPLETE without taking a look at selfishness. The self-absorbed we have always had with us, but today's society seems to have raised selfishness to an art form while giving it the seal of respectability.

The apex of American mythology has always been the rugged individualist, going his own way. But the unique factor along the American frontier, from the coastal colonies of the Atlantic to the closing of the frontier at the end of the nineteenth century, was the interdependence of neighbors.

Yes, scouts like Daniel Boone and Davy Crockett led the way over the eastern mountains through the vast dangerous forests of the era, but they always returned to their settlements for supplies and companionship. Settlement followed exploration. Neighbors banded together in their little clearings in the big woods to harvest crops, raise barns and fight off Indian incursions.

Just imagine neighbors in some suburb trying to get together to build even a birdhouse today.

America indeed was build on a concept of opportunity for the individual to go his own way and thrive, for unfettered free thought to build a new society in a new land. One of the negative things Americans seem good at is taking an essentially good idea and beating it into the ground. When rugged individualism becomes narcissistic self-involvement, that's what we've done.

Today's refrain is "I, I, I...Me, me, me."

I know I harp on the responsibilities of citizenship, but one excuse the self-absorbed give for not voting is that they are too busy making a living to take the time. I think our ancestors had us beat by miles in terms of "busy" when it comes to walking behind a mule all day turning stubborn soil, chopping firewood, and keeping their scalps. Yet they found time to vote.

That said, voting was a bit of a different thing back then. It was a break in backbreaking drudgery. You got to see your neighbors at the polling place. Maybe hear some rousing and entertaining speeches from the stump. You couldn't be accused of slacking off from clearing those bottoms or mending the harness, because voting was an important duty.

But it also was entertainment.

These days, we are up to our eyebrows in entertainment. And elections are boring. Community spirit in our pioneering days rose out of necessity. Out west, the cattle roundup was a community effort, where the fattened cattle were all housed together and then sorted by brand in the days before fencing. Small farmers took their produce to farmer's markets and exchanged gossip with other vendors and town-dwellers seeking their produce. Even a trip to the gristmill was a break, with stories spun and news caught up on.

Then came the industrial age and large smokestack industries to draw people away from the land and turn them into wage earners. Railroads brought remote sites closer, and Americans could go to the big city to seek their fortune. New Americans, arriving from other countries, expanded those industrial cities. But even within those cities, neighborhoods were essentially strings of small towns jammed together, and community spirit in a Brooklyn neighborhood was little different from that in Peoria, IL.

Then came the automobile, which to this day stands as a symbol of ultimate personal freedom. Just get in your car and go. Don't like Pittsburgh anymore? I hear they're hiring in Detroit. Or Cleveland. Or wherever.

Pursuit of a fatter paycheck or better climate became sufficient reason to uproot and go. If times turned tough, the answer was to head for greener pastures, as thousands of Okies did when they abandoned the Dust Bowl for California.

A natural consequence of this had to be the loss of a sense of community. Why involve yourself in local school boards, fire districts, and the like, when you are among strangers and probably won't be staying here more than a couple of years anyway? Why plant shade trees under which you will never sit? The focus became a restless quest for the better job, the new scene, the greener pasture.

Modern Day Daniel Boones

In a sense, the automobile returned to Americans a chunk of that Daniel Boone spirit. Americans sought the good life wherever their wheels could take them, through war, rumor of war, economic upturn and down. They may be politically apathetic, as I mention elsewhere, but they are indefatigable it seems in the pursuit of personal prosperity.

No less an observer of early America than Alexis de Tocqueville, that perceptive Frenchman, first identified this trait early in the history of the Republic. Ironically, it is de Tocqueville who is credited with coining the term "individualism." I say ironically, because he did not mean it in a complimentary way.

He saw Americans even then as constantly toiling to secure their comfortable futures, disinterested in the common good. These days, no matter how comfortable the present, more comforts are at hand. Just pay attention to the advertising barrage! De Tocqueville found Americans uncannily leery of simple leisure time, because they believed it led to melancholy.

A psychiatric observer might suggest that they ran as hard as they could to stay in one place—not unlike today's Americans—and feared contemplation because it might show a face of meaninglessness to the pursuit. Human nature really does have a hankering after a purpose, or meaning, according to present-day mind research.

Rather than confront the essential emptiness of a life spent in pursuit of more and more material gain, it seems we mount the treadmill again with a will, and with no energy left over to consider alternatives. Social ties are weak, and many people are lonely and somewhat at a loss.

The volatile mix of extreme preoccupation with individualism and the moral permissiveness that flowered in the 60s, in my view, are the sands upon which this national self indulgence is based. Divorce for just about any old reason has disintegrated so many of our families, as the former partners split in search of "their own thing"; it's no wonder that the lesson in selfishness was not lost on their impressionable offspring.

A culture war already is underway, fueled by the animosity of present wage earners against the retired and soon-to-be-retired who will count on social security. Rhetoric along the lines that today's wage earners are essentially wage slaves to the older generation is being heard across the land. This so-called war is sure to heat up as greying baby boomers begin to swell the rolls beyond all historical precedent, and social security coffers are threatened by long-lived retirees, thanks to present-day health care.

Greed vs. Politics

Another sign of self-absorption is less involvement in any aspect of our national political life, with all energies bent toward accumulating wealth. There is a widespread belief that enough money will insulate them from the vicissitudes of fortune, or even the toils of a stumbling government.

The selfish class, as I choose to style them, holds no conviction superior to their own economic determinism. For example, I recall a discussion with an individual who paid lip service to improving our air and water quality. He was bitter about what he perceived as the reluctance of major corporations to clean up their act. Then our conversation turned to investment. His stocks were doing quite well; interestingly, though, none in his portfolio were so-called "green" companies, or those committed to cleaning up the environment.

I asked him why not put his money where his mouth was, and transfer his investments to such companies. He was offended at the notion of surrendering his quite satisfactory rates of return for what he saw as the riskier growth potential of such stocks. Is it any wonder that profitable corporations forge right ahead, with environmental concerns held well below profitability? They know what their stockholders really want; they want return on investment!

Some observers are not as dismayed by all this selfishness as others. They point out that Americans have a long history of minding their own business. Some even believe our post-industrial society has returned in many ways to the pre-industrial society upon which de Tocqueville based his trenchant observations. De Tocqueville's America was decentralized, individualistic and property loving.

So are we today.

As for the gigantic federal government, many consider it to be an anachronistic irrelevance to their single-minded pursuit of more. Leaving government unwatched can be a mistake of calamitous proportions, which history would teach us—if we taught history!

Lost Sense of Community

Most of us were raised within the era of industrialism. Our sense of community survived the transition from rural agrarian America to the cities. Each neighborhood had its personality, as did our small towns and villages. Each community came equipped with social norms you broke only at risk of ostracism, and there were even busybodies to keep an eye on things. Like all things human, you took the bad with the good.

In the 40s, it was said that you didn't need to own a radio to follow "Amos N Andy," one of the most popular radio comedies. You could walk through your neighborhood on a summer's evening and hear every word on radios through open windows. The same was true of Cubs or Dodgers or Yankees games.

When the weather turned warm, houses remained hot inside long after evening temperatures had dropped, if only by a few degrees. In poorer neighborhoods, there weren't enough rooms for everyone anyway, so warm weather was an opportunity to spend time outdoors. You'd come home from work on the streetcar or el, and say "look, the neighborhood is out tonight." People talked to each other a lot then, and there was a lot of laughter too. The sense of community created that way was actually out of necessity, too—the necessity to get a breath of air outside the stultifying humidity of your home. It was a shared misery.

Today, you turn down a street and see doors standing open and lots of people out in the street and you think: "Trouble."

I think a lot of this changed perception may be traceable to technology; specifically air conditioning and television. Now you can be inside, cool and dry, freed from awful humidity. There on the screen are the talking pictures to keep you company. Not only that, the characters on the screen are wittier, smarter, and funnier than your neighbors could ever hope to be, thanks to the best screenwriters in the world.

Another plus is that the people on television won't come knocking on your door asking for a cup of sugar or a ride to the store. If you get tired of them, you just change the channel.

With all this technology, we have gained more comfort and more entertainment than our forefathers could have imagined after imbibing a quart of rum. But we lost our sense of community.

Consider My Life

I can point to my own life as an example. Because I have worked all-night shifts for many years, I mostly avoid the rush hours and other entanglements that are such irritants to modern life. No rush hour, no bosses present, no dress code. I can buy my groceries at 3 a.m. in a nearly deserted but open-for-business supermarket. Public parks and other facilities are uncrowded during the day when I get a chance to use them. My shopping companions during the day are young mothers and retirees. I seem to have found my own private frontier as surely as Daniel Boone. He and I would have different standards of how many people around us are too many, but the concept is the same.

How we value our neighbors seems to be in inverse ratio of how close we are required to live to them, and how many there are. Two miles away, where he is unlikely to interfere in my daily affairs unless asked? He's a great friend. Even two acres across there on his own large lot, and down the street, and all around the countryside, same thing. But next door, upstairs and underfoot, in an apartment building whose structure compels me to share his atonal East Indian music or her incessant rap, or the soulful caterwauling of a country western singer—hmm.

So you snug your earphones in place to shut out any evidence of other cultures too close to your own, light a scented candle to obscure cooking odors that don't appeal to you, and boot up your computer.

Our Virtual World

Perhaps in this land of closed physical frontiers, cyberspace will have to do for modern-day Daniel Boones with a yen for exploring. On the monitor, you can find virtual communities of like-minded persons, no matter what you want to talk about.

And if someone expresses an opinion that disturbs you, there's always the "ignore" click.

What I'm trying to get at here is that we cannot depend on outside forces to compel us back into a community spirit. We do see it emerge in times of natural disaster. Humans have spent thousands of years pulling together when the going gets rough, and a twister, hurricane, or flood can bring out the best in us. (And the worst, as in looters. A roving band of hooligans can pick us off one at a time, but if we are united like in the pioneer days, they wisely steer clear.)

Instead of waiting for outside circumstances, I suggest we consider making an effort to re-engage in our communities. Those neighbors might turn out to be pretty good folks. And who knows, you might be the one who one day needs a ride to the store.

Dirt Roads and Lost Identity

WHILE WORKING ON THIS BOOK, I READ A LOT OF MATERIAL — from books by professors about our lost civility to myriad online offerings about various issues of concern to syndicated columnists. A number of points caught my eye that don't fit tidily into one or another of my chapters, but that I feel are worthy of mention and consideration. I hope you will agree.

Dirt Roads

Paul Harvey, my radio colleague, has made the following rather profound observation:

"What's mainly wrong with society today is that too many Dirt Roads have been paved. There's not a problem in America today, crime, drugs, education, divorce, delinquency that wouldn't be remedied, if we just had more Dirt Roads, because Dirt Roads give character. People that live at the end of Dirt Roads learn early on that life is a bumpy ride. That it can jar you right down to your teeth sometimes, but it's worth it, if at the end is home…a loving spouse, happy kids and a dog. We wouldn't have near the trouble with our educational system if our kids got their exercise walking a Dirt Road with other kids, from whom they learn how to get along.

"There was less crime in our streets before they were paved. Criminals didn't walk two dusty miles to rob or rape, if they knew they'd be welcomed by 5 barking dogs and a double barrel shotgun. And there were no drive by shootings. Our values were better when our roads were worse! People did not worship their cars more than their kids, and motorists were more courteous, they didn't tailgate by riding the bumper or the guy in front would choke you with dust & bust your windshield with rocks. Dirt Roads taught patience. Dirt Roads were environmentally friendly, you didn't hop in your car for a quart of milk you walked to the barn for your milk. For your mail, you walked to the mailbox. What if it rained and the Dirt Road got washed out? That was the best part, then you stayed home and had some family time, roasted marshmallows and popped popcorn and pony road on Daddy's shoulders and learned how to make prettier quilts than anybody.

"At the end of Dirt Roads, you soon learned that bad words tasted like soap. Most paved roads lead to trouble, Dirt Roads more likely lead to a fishing creek or a swimming hole. At the end of a Dirt Road, the only time we even locked our car was in August, because if we didn't some neighbor would fill it with too much zucchini. At the end of a Dirt Road, there was always extra springtime income, from when city dudes would get stuck, you'd have to hitch up a team and pull them out. Usually you got a dollar…always you got a new friend…at the end of a Dirt Road."

Brand Name Identity

To know what our country is and may become, we need to look at who we are and what we are becoming. While I keep holding out for our identity as citizens of a free society, we more commonly today are classified as "consumers."

The business of America has always seemed to be business, as the fictional Babbitt remarked years ago. Business means selling something, and selling requires buyers. That's us.

In simpler times, any good-size town in American usually could boast two bakeries, two newspapers, two supermarkets, two dairies, two and sometimes three mail-order centers for the major department store chains. (Sears Roebuck, Penneys and "Monky" Ward.)

You were either a Ford man or a Chrysler man or a General Motors man. At the middle-class level, you drove your Ford or Plymouth or Chev to one of the two supermarkets and purchased milk from one of the two dairies and bread from one of the two bakeries (never the other!)

You subscribed to one of the two newspapers. And you probably either had Coke or Pepsi—seldom both—in your refrigerator.

Each of these choices defined us to ourselves, helped us establish our identity.

Such choices still do, and the marketing mavens gather this information on us with the devotion of an archaeologist in the throne chamber of a newly discovered pyramid.

As local and regional dairies, and supermarkets, and bakeries, and newspapers began to be gobbled up and homogenized larger and larger acquisition drives, a sort of sameness developed. White bread was white bread, Vitamin D milk was Vitamin D milk, despite the color of the carton.

All of this activity coincided with the rise of Madison Avenue as the focal point of American advertising, and the application of psychological principles to selling stuff.

Enter "branding."

Branding is a business strategy to sell you emotional baggage and a sense of identity, not just the product. Companies are trying to sell you nostalgic roots back to your own roots and theirs; or a sense of their social responsibility; or persuade us that this pair of hiking boots will turn us into lean, flexible high-trail hikers.

If I mention L. L. Bean, I bet a buck you will think of the rugged New England spirit first, and second, of a company with a long history of standing behind its products. Nike? "Just do it!"

Step back from consumerism for a moment.

I've seen reports from cultural anthropologists who say we, as Americans, don't much like or trust our government these days. Same goes for school administrations, or the various churches which were once repositories of almost unquestioning trust. The news media may be a little more trusted than used-car salesmen but I bet it's a close finish.

So in whom do we place our trust? Brand-name marketers hope it will be their products. A strong, reliable product backed by "branding" of the company as trustworthy and full of integrity.

Has it really come to this?

Have we reached the point where all we can believe in is the advertising rhetoric behind outrageously expensive sneakers or boutique coffee? Where as never before, we are what we drive, or wear, or bathe our bodies with?

If all it takes to achieve this new loyalty is the slick copywriting skills of advertising experts, perhaps it's time our government, our churches, our schools, our public libraries looked to their advertising budgets.

"It's your conviction. Just vote it!"

Identity and Privacy

There has been a good deal of publicity lately about scam artists who steal our very identity and credit rating to run up large debts, and the difficulty a victim then has in reclaiming his or her good name.

There have always been scam artists, and of course they would adapt, probably faster than the rest of us, to credit cards and the Internet. There is enough legitimate business being done over computers today that there is a vested interest in curtailing these activities, and I think they will be curtailed. In the meantime, most authorities advise vigilance and caution.

Okay so far. What caught my eye is something a little more fundamental. While we are all advised to guard our personal social security number, I came across a syndicated column by Jane Bryant Quinn that reports that doing so is frequently beyond our control. Up until the late 1990s, she reports, anyone could buy any social security number right over the Internet. Then the Federal Trade Commission and Congress persuaded the "database entry" to halt such widespread marketing.

However, commercial firms, lawyers, private detectives, debt collectors, phone companies, hospital and insurance companies, and employers and police still may purchase them, she said.

Which to my mind is a loophole so large the general prohibition is almost meaningless. What defines a "commercial firm" for instance? Incorporation? A business license? And the regulation of private detectives is far from uniform across this nation.

The social security number is the key element in identity theft. And Quinn's conclusion was that under present law, you are essentially helpless to protect it.

The underlying force behind this wholesaling of the SSN? Why, marketing, of course. A theme I have reiterated several times is that everything seems to be for sale today. Including your privacy and peace of mind.

It will stay that way until we, the people, say we've had enough.

Speaking of privacy and ownership, do we own our own names anymore?

Recently, published authors found their names being purloined by "cybersquatters." (A squatter is someone who buys up an Internet "domain" name such as those ending in .org, .com or .net and then offers to sell the name back to its owner at whatever the market will bear.)

I heard of one case while preparing this book where a "squatter" purchased the domain name of a toy company and then threatened to offer porn over the net in that name unless the toy company came through with a fat purchase price to buy its name back. To me, that's just plain extortion.

Maybe you're not famous, but your name should belong to you!

I know a lot of us bear the same name, and that's bound to lead to some confusion. I did a cursory online check and came up with 13 other Jim Bohannons! But that's not what I'm talking about.

I also heard of a case from the other side of the issue, where a small legitimate company named VirtualWorks wanted "VW.com." Volkswagen of America was having none of that, and prevailed, though the small company filed first. Long-established advertising law about trademarks and copyright infringement evidently came into play.

But just in case, there is a new federal law, passed in 1999, called the Anticybersquatting Consumer Protection Act (ACPA) which is part of the Intellectual Property & Communications Omnibus Reform Act of 1999. This law prohibits bad-faith registration or use of a domain name that is the intellectual property of another party. You can invoke this law to enjoin (and punish) such use of your name.

I think this whole issue of our names and personal information being bandied about by "database companies" or anybody else needs a serious overview. We are more than just potential consumers; we are citizens!

CHAPTER 6

Apathy

IN MY RADIO TALK SHOW, I OFTEN HEAR FROM EXTREMISTS OF ALL STRIPES, from the far right to the far left.

They love the idea of getting on the air to espouse this or that viewpoint, and defend it with the tenacity of a high school debating student.

I am a seeker for the voice of reasonableness. An extremist in defense of the middle way, if you will. A believer that compromise lies at the heart of democratic process, where everybody's ox is gored, but none too much.

But I have to say this for the extremists: they do espouse some cause or other, even if they do it at the top of their voices. They do put in the time to call, they do put in the time to exchange views over the Internet, they attend town hall meetings, and they write their elected officials. They know the squeaky wheel gets the grease.

And so we enter the era of political correctitude.

The Politically Correct

Indians become "Native Americans" even though they're really only "earliest immigrant Americans." Chairmen become chairpersons. The comedian, George Carlin, has made a career by making us laugh until we cry with his variations on such political correctitude. Sadly, only comedians seem able to speak on such things without being borne under by the sheer weight of ultra liberal disapproval.

In today's society where civics lessons have been foresworn and critical thinking skills phased out, there seems no reasonable place to stand. Civilized discourse needs a fulcrum before conflict can be levered into reasonable compromise.

But just try to take a position on anything, and some special-interest group will rise up, feelings all offended, to swat you down. Our history has been sanitized, "corrected politically," airbrushed retroactively to fit abstract but inaccurate concepts.

We used to laugh at the Kremlin in Soviet Union days when Politburo members who fell out of favor were airbrushed out of May Day reviewing stand photos.

But the whole history and bedrock principles of this nation seem to have been smoothed out of our awareness.

It's not surprising that so much of our population has surrendered to apathy. When your opinions or values are swept aside by those professing a superior knowledge of how things should be, you either give up or go to the extreme to fight back. Most give up.

Our Apathetic Young

The younger generation seems to inherit this apathy. They become almost passive. I think this wave of apathy is traceable to our nation's public schools. For at least four decades, our schools have failed to drum into young heads civics lessons about how this nation is supposed to work. School programs seem to strive to program kids into conformist roles. Education in how to think critically and skeptically is significantly missing.

When kids are spewed out of this conveyor belt into everyday life, they can be excused for thinking they don't really matter as individuals. Nothing's going to change, it doesn't matter anyway and the whole effort of even thinking about such things is boring. Let's play a video game or head for the beach.

Hard on the heels of the baby boomers in our progression of generations are the 30-somethings. Not quite old enough to have been hippies and go to San Francisco with flowers in their hair, they were children then. The highly publicized party days of the 60s, and attendant activism, left a mark on them. By the time they were into their teens, though, the blah 70s had arrived, bringing with it Nixon and Watergate, the fall of Saigon, double-knit leisure suits and a general confusion about the place of America in the world.

Activism lost its impetus when civil rights moved into the mainstream with affirmative action programs and left the streets and freedom marches. The antiwar movement dissolved with no more war to be against. Somehow ecological protests and anti-nuclear protests and prison reform protests didn't generate the same fever.

The party was over.

The flower children had matured, rested from their labors and shifted their attention to personal gain. They would become the advance guard for the Greedy 80s. "Greed is good" and "he who dies with the most toys wins" would become their mottos.

The 30-somethings of today dutifully went off to college to make something of themselves in the 70s, and began to arrive in the workforce about the time of the 1980s downsizing and "rightsizing" hit American enterprise. Tens of thousands of baby boomers, then in their 40s, were turned out into the streets to compete with the next generation for a dwindling pool of jobs. Corporations took entire production operations offshore to avoid American labor costs.

The 30-somethings found that their political science or philosophy degrees were essentially useless as they were forced into retail sales in mall stores or flipping burgers at the Golden Arches. It is only in the recent boom years that they finally are finding their stride.

Meanwhile, the "X" generation was coming on, observing the often fruitless struggles of the ones just ahead of them—and sinking into apathy.

Perhaps it's a cycle; in the prosperous post-war 1950s there was a "beat" generation; now there's the "slacker" Xers, approaching their own big three-O.

And the "Y" generation (as in, why bother?) is in the wings.

These are kids who have been locked up in school part of the day, forced to sit in rows, controlled and patrolled by X-ray machines and armed guards.

If their general demeanor resembles that of sullen prisoners, is that any surprise?

But the massive apathy, all by itself, is cause for concern. If a majority of our citizens believe they can have no effect on how things work in our democracy, doesn't that become a self-fulfilling prophecy?

Docility and a Thriving System

As I point out in my chapter on politics, there are plenty of well-heeled political action committees perfectly happy to determine the course of the nation to suit themselves, absent interference from a docile populace.

I have to admit such docility may also be an earmark of a society that is working fairly well. Passivity could be the by-product of a successful, thriving system.

When things are working well overall, and problems facing most of us are relatively minor, such as whether to take that Tahiti vacation or buy a new car—in other words, as long as it doesn't affect me, who cares?—there is no incentive to get involved or take concerted action.

As for the less fortunate, they are more or less out of sight, out of mind.

It is all well and good to talk about altruism, or doing good for the sake of doing good, but human beings are pleasure seekers first and last, and what's the payback for doing good? For becoming involved? For stepping out of the cozy cocoon of normalcy to rub shoulders with the unbathed, the hungry, the hopeless?

Abstract concepts like laying up treasures in heaven for your good works on earth, or the more esoteric view that we become better people by acting better, don't appeal to the apathetic.

"No good deed goes unpunished" seems to be the motto of the day. So why seek out punishment?

Take politics as an example.

Most of us seem unwilling to sit through an hour-long Presidential debate on where this country should be going. We pretty much don't care, as long as it's not in our neighborhood. The fact that it might come to our neighborhood, and by then it will be too late, requires analytic thinking. That's too much bother.

The gubernatorial election that got everybody talking, and beat all others for sheer entertainment value, was the one in Minnesota where Jesse "The Body" Ventura captured the state house. Ventura is a born entertainer, a celebrity who knows how to work the crowds. He stirred their amusement and interest, and upset the system mightily.

Seems the only thing that can penetrate apathy is entertainment.

I sometimes think that if our Presidential elections were going to get any attention at all, candidates like Bush and Gore would have to engage in a nationally televised laser-lighted mud-wrestling contest. (Real gooey mud, not the pallid political kind.)

I have talked with people who place no value on their right to vote. If someone came along and offered them free health care to surrender it, I don't think they would hesitate.

Each of the precious Bill of Rights, a concept that set the United States apart from the rest of the world, would, I fear, be traded away if the incentive were appealing enough. In fact, a recent poll by Rasmussen Research of Charlotte, NC, found only 51 percent of adults polled would vote for the US Constitution! Twenty-two percent would vote against it! Almost as frightening is that 27 percent couldn't or wouldn't decide.

Put another way, if repeal of any of them were put to the test, would our populace be sufficiently motivated to vote to protect them?

Who's the group most likely to vote in this country?

Older Voters Make a Difference

Our older citizens, that's who. They have something at stake in what they have accumulated over their life's work. They're the ones who most often vote 'no' in school bond issues and anything that smacks of raised taxes. Their kids are raised, and they're husbanding their resources for their dotage. With their 'no' votes, they seem to be saying that a lack of community spirit is not confined to the young or to the harried wage-earner.

A popular saying once was that in our youth we're all Democrats, but as we age we turn Republican. Some would say the shift to conservatism appears as soon as we get our first paycheck and see how much dough has been whacked out of it by the government.

Are we free wage-earners, or indentured servants to the national debt? When times are less economically flush than they were at the turn of this century, that's not really an apocryphal question. It has some impact.

When we learn for instance that our telephone bills as late as 1999 were still assessing us a "temporary" tax to finance the Spanish-American War, we are first scandalized and then resigned. What can we do? Nothing, we seem to conclude, and write the check, though Teddy Roosevelt's charge up San Juan Hill has been in the history books for an awful long time.

These days there is a certain nostalgia for the activism of the 60s.

Greying baby boomers wax poetic over the things they accomplished as young men and women, whether or not they ever rode a freedom bus. There was idealism, yes. And perhaps there were sparks of achievement here and there. But the period was far from a simon-pure demonstration of interest in the greater good. It was one large decade-long party. Young people turned on, tuned in and dropped out. Along the way, some of them marched for civil rights. The rest played their music too loud, wore their hair too long, and maintained an air of moral superiority to the rest of us who went to war or followed traditional values.

But if activism involved going into a cane field to cut sugarcane all day, sitting all day at a desk doling out funds to the needy, or cleaning up garbage in a ghetto, how many would show up?

Lost Generations

We have raised several generations now without much of an attention span, conditioned to sound bites and with the channel changer always ready at hand. Their babysitter was a TV, and their schooling was similar to prison. Silent conformity was the way to slide by, and they slid. If they wish for anything much, it's probably a channel clicker for life in general, so that if something is upsetting or not entertaining enough—click. Gone.

From the 60s on, I believe, we have had no solid educational basis of what a democracy entails and what our responsibilities as citizens are. Universities and colleges have ironed out our American history, rewriting it, squeezing out the blood and thunder and the glory. It has been "politically corrected."

We wind up agonizing over whether it's okay to teach unexpurgated Mark Twain. Students with no training in history, civics or civility, exposed to the everyday language of Twain's time, might very well turn to a classmate and use the infamous "N" word. Didn't the famous author use it?

What about the trick Huck's aunt used to catch him when he was dressed up in girls' clothing? She tossed something in his lap. He automatically shut his knees to catch it. She crowed in triumph because a girl would have spread her legs to catch it in her skirt. (And what would the politically correct say about THAT?)

Are We Too Preoccupied?

What to do? Airbrush our literature, too?

One of the most compelling forces that breeds apathy is the simple fact that most of us are too tied down by the mechanics of making a living, paying bills, and staying afloat to take an interest in our community or the world around us. I've talked elsewhere about how much is enough, and the constant din of advertising which reinforces this debt-incurring cycle.

When we focus only on a new washer and dryer, new car, the latest computer games for the kids, we are shortchanging not only our families by not having time for them, but our communities. They are shortchanged by expectations that they will run themselves and maintain their strengths, the very strengths that we rely upon and often take for granted.

Some of the more cynical would say that our free-market system is designed to keep our citizens isolated from each other in pursuit of their own comfort and gain. I think it's just a result of poor planning and not taking the broad view.

Civic clubs and other non-profit organizations can do a world for good for us all. Think how much good could be accomplished if all of us bestirred ourselves to join just one such enterprise?

Why bother?

Well, enlightened self-interest might serve where pure altruism won't. If you are a member of the Lion's Club or the Rotary or a church group or any other organization engaged in worthy causes, you will find abundant opportunity to "network," hand out your business card, make yourself and your abilities known community wide. You trade your altruism for potential personal gain. I have no problem with that at all. It's a free trade concept that works for the common good, and for yours.

Following my belief that the government and its tax structure should have as one of its purposes the nudging of citizens in the direction of right action, perhaps it's time to simplify a tax break for the working man or woman who will donate time to worthy causes.

A lot of decrepit housing could be made livable, a lot of playgrounds fixed up, a lot of the hungry fed, if all of us could mobilize to the task for just one day a week away from our own selfish concerns, our jacuzzis, and our Internet.

CHAPTER 7

The Family

THIS NATION OF OURS WAS CREATED IN REVOLUTION, tempered in civil war and expanded coast to coast by a mutually perceived "manifest destiny" of greatness. Out of these tumultuous beginnings we developed a rock-solid foundation of belief about who we were and where we were going. Much of that foundation rested squarely on our families. People got married and stayed married, and had lots of children. The children pitched in to keep the family fed and clothed as soon as they were old enough. They learned their values and their sense of self within the framework of the family, and used those values and self-knowledge when they left home to build their own families.

Toughing It Out in the Early Days

Life was far from rosy in those early days. This continent was largely a wilderness. Its original inhabitants were viewed as savages. American Indian tribes were shoved aside and demonized. Blacks were first enslaved and then segregated. Politically, women were second class citizens, without even the right to vote. But the Constitutional mechanisms created in Philadelphia by our Founding Fathers, under the guiding principle of a rule of law and not of men, were eventually used to correct most of these imbalances. In a perfect world, all would have been corrected long since. But the process is ongoing.

From the end of the eighteenth and through the nineteenth centuries, the unique character that the world came to call an American was formed: God-fearing, hard-working, adventurous, optimistic, industrious, innovative, freedom-loving and entrepreneurial. Ours was a frontier spirit, full of hope, and it kindled a spark in the hearts of men and women from every part of the globe. To this day, the ringing pronouncements about the inalienable rights of man forged by our founders are emulated by emerging nations, whether there is any intention of living up to them or not. The concept of a government of the people, for the people and by the people raised the bar of human expectations on a global scale.

Where does all this leave the American family today?

The American family was the cornerstone to development of that essential American character. The family was the essential social unit of our culture. Explorers might venture alone into the great wilderness, but families soon followed. Pioneer sons toted their own muzzleloaders to add to the larder and defend the family unit; pioneer daughters labored shoulder to shoulder with their mothers.

As settlements grew, families labored together on the land. The social unit also was a cohesive economic unit. Large families meant more hands to turn to the tasks—and a hedge against the deadly diseases of the day that decimated so many young people prematurely. In a family of seven children, it was not unusual for two or three to never reach maturity. Families dealt with these tragedies the best way they could, and persevered. These families joined in communities, from crossroads villages to prospering cities, and exercised their American rights to life, liberty and the pursuit of happiness, free of government oppression. Well into the twentieth century, the most familiar symbol of the federal government to the everyday citizen was the Post Office letter carrier—a servant of the people, not a boss.

Industry Transforms the Family

The Industrial Revolution provoked a migration away from traditional communities and into larger and larger concentrations within industrial cities. Living conditions often were poor. There were plenty of doomsayers then who predicted this shift from agrarianism to industrialism would ruin the American way of life. An industrialized nation was more interested in bodies to man the machines than in the family that supported those bodies. Sweat shops and labor strife, robber barons and monopolies were some of the trademarks of the period.

But American family life survived, and adapted.

Big city tenements and neighborhoods developed their own character, often close-knit in the face of new adversities, often emulative of the communities left behind. Wave after wave of immigrants swelled the ranks of the urban working class, and fought their own battles for acceptance in this turbulent nation. There still are people alive who remember "NINA" signs: "No Irish Need Apply."

Poor wages and lousy living conditions, discrimination of all sorts, poor food and ravaging disease—through it all, the American dream survived. The Depression was tough—damn tough. And there were two World Wars. That industrial might which had been the boogey man of the doomsayers was used by this nation to thwart the international designs of totalitarian regimes. Mass-produced weaponry in the hands of the sons of Americans from all walks of life defeated the forces of those dictators who would have turned back the clock on human rights, perhaps for keeps.

Back then, someone had said that the surest way for Americans to win a war was to draft its young men away from their families and everyday pursuits, inform them that they were in "for the duration," and then point at some objective—say Berlin or Tokyo—and tell them when you've secured that, you can go home. Didn't matter how unlikely the objective was. Just point 'em at it and tell 'em when they had conquered it they could go home.

The proof was in the performance.

At the end of the Second World War, America bestrode the planet like a true Colossus. No nation had ever been more powerful. Steel-pot-wearing Kilroys had conquered the Nazis and Imperial Japan, inscribed their famous moniker everywhere, liberated the death camps and freed the survivors of the Death March. The Coke and a Zippo lighter were universal icons of a can-do nation. America stood in a fair position to impose a "pax Americana" on the world at the end of that war, much as had Rome and the British Empire in previous eras.

But Americans by and large tend to mind their own business.

They won the big war—and went home. Rosie the Riveter put aside her coveralls and married Kilroy, and they used the GI Bill to buy homes and get married and go to college. They fueled a postwar prosperity that still reverberates today as their offspring reach the grey-templed years. America marched steadily on into the brave new world of air conditioning, color TV and two cars in every garage. "Father Know Best" and "Ozzie and Harriet" seemed to epitomize the period. It would have been forgivable somewhere along in there to suggest that "happily ever after" had arrived.

But the fairy tale ended.

The 60s Upheaval of the Family

The Civil Rights Movement demanded redress of long-time wrongs. Reaction from some quarters was violent. Domestic strife again became the order of the day. TV images of fire hoses and police dogs loosed on peaceful demonstrators shook our complacency. Assassins struck down larger-than-life political figures. Cities burned. Young people began to question everything in the 1960s. A whole generation of our children became estranged from our core values, wondering indeed if those values had every existed. Generational tensions soared.

Onto this inflammatory mix was poured the gasoline of the Vietnam war, hugely divisive in ways no other American conflict but our Civil War had been. Our already-rebellious young people poured blood on draft board files, burned their draft cards, marched in protest or fled to Canada. Hell no, they weren't going! The ones who did go faced the most un-American way of combat: just survive a year in "Nam," and you can call it a day, go home to the land of the round door knob, and try to sleep at night. When they did return, they were often greeted with scorn as baby killers. When they didn't…well, in previous wars, a gold star in a family's window was held in highest respect—a son had sacrificed his life for our nation. By and large, there was no such respect for the war dead of Vietnam, or for the grief of their families.

Over and above all this was the steady, unrelenting pressure of the Cold War and the specter of "mutually assured destruction" via nuclear arms. "Better Red than Dead" became a catch phrase of the day, suggesting there were no other choices in the matter. There was a strong sense that you might as well live for today, do your "own thing" right now, this moment, because tomorrow might never come. The stubborn insistence to keep fighting by older Americans in the halls of power, as they locked horns around the globe with what Reagan ultimately named the "Evil Empire," only made for more distrust among the young. Anyone could see that a brawling, sprawling, undisciplined nation such as ours was no match for the disciplined ruthlessness of the Soviet state.

Anyone was wrong, of course, and before the twentieth century waned, we won the Cold War too.

But the victory took its dreadful toll.

The Civil War, the Industrial Revolution, the Great Depression— none of these huge societal convulsions had managed to break the succession of values from generation to generation. The Cold War and the 1960s did.

As the old issues which so bitterly divided the 1960s young from their elders went away, and as they grew older and had children of their own, a vacuum seemed to develop. A vacuum of passed-down values. Into the vacuum stepped the free market, both legal and illegal, offering all new and better toys to divert the newly self-centered citizens (and their offspring) of our land. From junk bonds to nose candy, everything was pitched for immediate gratification. The transfer of traditional family values from generation to generation was so severely disrupted that all that seemed left was to keep on "doing your own thing." Is it any wonder that this became the lesson for the children of the 1980s and 1990s?

The Family Disintegrates

Doing your own thing, for parents, means splitting up over just about anything. It seems easier to divorce than stay married these days. Divorce has easy to follow steps, and a legion of lawyers to guide you. Marriage comes with no owner's manual, and is damned hard work sometimes. When gratification goes, it's time to think about "doing your own thing" with the new romantic interest, or going off to seek your true destiny somewhere over the rainbow.

Divorce has reached epidemic proportions. Women sometimes choose to have children without a husband around, or even a permanent live in partner. Sometimes it seems they want a child like they want a puppy. But you can't take the child back to the pound when it gets troublesome.

So many children today come from single-parent or "blended" or "complicated" families. (Don't you love euphemisms for step-parents and live-in lovers?) Often the single parent is a mother, struggling to make ends meet. One statistic I saw indicates that of 5.7 million women who are single heads of households, only half got the child support to which they were entitled, and 25 percent of them got nothing at all!

Dad must be too busy financing his own thing.

The Plight of Single-Parent Households

Such single-parent households have grown by almost 50 percent in this country. That's millions and millions of children without two parents looking after them. Latch-key kids, while Mom struggles to keep food on the table and a roof over their heads.

Is this growth significant? You bet it is. Educational studies show that the advent of the single-parent household is the single largest stumbling block to academic success as children enter the school system. Even though children by and large are better nourished, healthier, and materially better off than in previous generations, all these gains are negated by the absence of a two-parent family.

Research papers in the early 1990s looked at Indochinese "boat people" who arrived in this country after literally years of physical and emotional trauma. They couldn't speak English, they were broke and most adults were poorly educated. They gravitated to low-income inner cities and sent their children to schools with poor track records.

But their children excelled.

Not just a few—the majority.

The reason? The emotional support and high expectations of their stalwart and close-knit family units. The very same attributes upon which this nation was founded!

Remember those old slogans like the family that prays (or plays) together stays together? I think I'd settle for a family that sits down to dinner together at least a couple of times a week.

Back when the family was a cohesive social and economic unit, the business of family living was often transacted over the dinner table. To this day, state-funded group homes for dysfunctional teens find that required attendance at meals fosters bonding and a sense of shared values among the most shattered of children. Think how much more powerful this effect might be on families if parents insisted on such gatherings again! Our newest Americans never stopped doing it. It's time for the rest of us to go back to such basics too, or we stand a chance to lose yet another generation to confusion and sloth.

I may get jumped on for this comparison, but children are like wolves; they socialize to the pack. Don't believe it? Then why do so many inner-city kids from shattered homes wind up as fiercely loyal gang members, willing to pay whatever dues in blood or atrocity are required? Ready to kill or die to belong.

To me this is proof that kids will accept a system, almost any system, provided they understand it is a system, and understand their place in that system. The family provides a hierarchy into which the young person can fit and develop until he or she is ready to leave that environment and strike out to build a hierarchy of their own.

Schools as Surrogate Family?

In my chapter on dumbing down, I talked about schools becoming almost a surrogate for the family failures. But programs like the famous Head Start only provide momentary spikes in the learning potential of those children, according to the latest reports. Head Start kids generally sink back to the mean level of achievement (or lack of it) once they have left such programs. Loss of momentum seems to occur from the first day. It's like giving me a quarter-mile head start on a trained marathoner; he's still going to run me in the ground without breaking a sweat, because of his coaches and his daily training and the expectations of his support group.

For children, that support system needs to be a family. A family consists of adult role models who take responsibility for guiding children, for spending time with them, for such simple but crucial tasks as reading aloud to them. Taking them to the zoo, or to the fishing pier, or bird watching. In the vernacular of today, "being there" for them.

Children need to bond with what social workers call their "primary care provider."

Fifteen minutes of "quality time" with Mom between work and her aerobics workout isn't going to do it.

The evidence is in, nationwide. Nothing can replace the hours and hours that mothers and fathers used to spend with their offspring. As a society, we face some tough decisions. The rulers of the workplace need to make allowances, as they demand more and more time from their employees, for the presence of children onsite. A "take your kid to work" day once a year is just tokenism. Having access to your children on breaks during the work day needs to be the norm.

As parents, we need to make decisions too. First and foremost, if you are considering parenthood, realize it's the toughest task you'll ever face. If you aren't dedicated to bringing it off, haven't thought it through completely and asked yourself at least a hundred realistic questions about what it will be like and what you'll do in this or that situation—don't do it! Devote the time you can to the children of your siblings or other family members, or of friends and neighbors. It still does take a village to raise a child, and your contribution to youth that way can be vital.

If you're determined to have children—or already have them—you need to decide just what "having it all" means in terms of your family. I'd like to think that having it all means a balanced and healthy family relationship, rather than big-screen TVs and dirt bikes. If you can swing some of the fancier toys, fine—but that shouldn't be the focus. Whether kids will come right out and say it or not, my hunch is that they often consider such gadgets bribes paid to avoid spending too much time with them. Being as self-centered as you, they'll take 'em, sure.

But will those things ever, ever replace the time you could have spent with them watching them grow, watching their wonder as you show them the world through your eyes and watch them begin to see it through their own? As you help them learn to reason and interact with the world around them, and make their own choices about things?

My answer is a resounding "no!"

The Future of the Family

When you consider the present trends, I worry a lot about just how children are going to find their way to adulthood. Projections I have read indicate that high divorce rates, cohabitation and single parenthood will eventually mean that the majority of children in this country will not experience a childhood that includes the original two parents. Already, mature adults are crying out "where are my grandchildren?" as their own offspring shy away from marriage and family.

Some studies suggest that the only way to maintain a stable population—and workforce—in this nation will be if the immigrants keep coming. The face of America will keep changing and changing until it is unrecognizable.

There is much talk these days about "family values." I'd like to turn that phrase around a little. We as a society need to value families. In an economy where the individual worker is the economic unit at one end of the equation, and the individual consumer at the other, even couples who want to marry and raise a traditional family face an uphill battle. Remember the vicious political fights over legislation creating "family leave?" Much of the rhetoric was couched in terms of lost productivity—the economic argument again.

Can you imagine the arguments if legislation were introduced to require employers to excuse employees to attend their children's baseball games and piano recitals? Brother! But doesn't that send a message that the family, and the growth of its children, are irrelevant to production? I simply don't believe that's true in the first place, and even if it were, what should our nation worry more about producing: stable families, or a few more units of this or that consumable good?

Must everything be for sale in this country then—even the family? Maybe it's time for families to become a special-interest group, with lobbyists and political action groups of their own. Tax laws need to be overhauled to create incentives for independent families—not incentives for welfare recipients. Housing costs need to be brought under control somehow; right now, if two young parents want to own a home in which to raise children, it is almost certain both will have to work outside that home—and their kids will see it on weekends and to sleep, and spend the rest of their non-education time in daycare. Or become latchkey kids, being babysat by the boob tube.

One thing's for sure: if we let things keep going the way they're going, the path is clearly all downhill as far as giving the basic American family a valued place in the scheme of things is concerned.

If you are among those who yearn for a marriage with kids, a place of your own, and some time to develop as a family, it's time to find others of like mind and make your feelings known loud and clear to the politicians. Special interests in this country always have the ear of the politicians—sad but true. Only when you become a force to be reckoned with in your own right can you expect to see the powers-that-be begin to take a re-emergence of American core values seriously. The wheel that squeaks gets the grease. It's time for mothers and fathers, and those who aspire to be, and for those of us who grew up in those better times and know the value of a family in our own emotional formation, to stand up and be counted.

I don't claim to have all the answers. But I know in my heart that children need a family—mother, father, aunts, uncles, grandparents, and yes, neighbors too—to help shape their perceptions of the world and guide them toward a healthy relationship with this complicated world of ours.

If we can swing our cultural values back that way, I see a rebirth of the American as ideal citizen: exuberant, confident, can-do.

And it's something we really can do.

CHAPTER 8

Poverty

ONE OF THE ENDURING ISSUES FACING OUR NATION IS THAT OF POVERTY. In this we are not unique by any means; every civilized society has had and continues to have its underclass. "The poor we will always have with us" is one of those truisms beyond dispute. In a nation based on the wide-open competition of the free marketplace, there will always be winners—and losers.

Where America is unique is that we were the first nation to have the temerity to declare "war" on poverty, as if it were a specific enemy to be defeated by the mobilization of our national resources. President Lyndon B. Johnson sounded the call to arms early in his administration. Contemporary historians suggest that the battle plans were already being laid by the Kennedy administration, and holdover officials from that administration, in the numbed days after Kennedy's assassination, approached Johnson with the idea.

Until the Johnson declaration of war, all societies heretofore had just sort of accepted that there would always be the poor. Lamentable, but just the way of things.

In order to meet an enemy, you have to define it...and in America, poverty was defined by certain threshold incomes. In the years since the 60s, we keep redefining poverty. If, for instance, you define poverty as the 20 percent of the population making the least amount of money, poverty never seems to go away or be diminished. With inflation and other factors, what would have been a fine income in the 60s is dirt-poor now.

There is poverty, and then there's poverty. If you had a TV set in the 60s, you weren't considered poor. That's pretty much gone by the way-side now. TVs are cheaper for one thing, relative to income. And what about a microwave? Is it a convenience, or a necessity? If you see a mi-crowave as an appliance for getting the popcorn to pop so you can watch your favorite TV show, maybe that's one thing. But if it's a way to get warm breakfast for your kids before both of you rush off to minimum wage jobs to try to keep a roof over your heads, that's quite another.

Still, even if it is the latter, perhaps three-quarters of the world we live in would see such American "poverty" as something like middle-class.

I've seen poverty up close, poverty with a capital P.

Early in my Vietnam military tour, I was assigned to the garbage de-tail for our 50-man detachment. The driver and I loaded four 50-gallon drums of garbage into a 3/4-ton pickup and headed for the dump area. As we reached the dump, the driver warned me to roll up the windows and lock the doors, as he slowed to 25 mph.

Then I saw the children converging like rapacious wolves.

They swarmed into the back of the truck before it had come to a com-plete halt, fighting each other viciously for the contents of the drums.

Almost in the time it takes to tell it, they scattered again, leaving the drums overturned in the back of the truck. When we turned the cans up again, they were empty. Utterly empty. Even the fat slugs that col-lected on our banana peels had been taken.

That's poverty.

A friend of mine spent time in Asmara, Ethiopia, during the famine. Each day, a "body detail" would be out early in the morning to collect those who didn't make it through the night. Literally starved to death.

That's poverty.

Against this, does a rent-controlled apartment, even with thin walls, seem so bad? Even if the TV doesn't work and you have to use the con-ventional oven for meals? If you have a roof, and food, and basic cloth-ing, you at least are surviving. Heat in the winter, and yes, cooling in the summer too, especially in the overcrowded inner cities, where heat exhaustion and heat stroke can be real threats to life.

Beyond the essentials for life, a lot of what we call poverty is what I call "manufactured pain." What do I mean by this? I mean the desire for a vast array of consumables generated by a constant din of advertising on every level. Now I may sound like I'm biting the hand that feeds me, because most of my life, my income has been derived from advertising sales. And suppliers of goods and services have a perfect right to advertise their wares.

Where I would like to draw the line is in the "how" of advertising, in which canny behaviorists plot campaigns designed to make us feel life is just not worth living without designer jeans, cell phones and hot tubs. Every supplier of goods is competing fiercely for an after-all finite number of dollars from we the consumers, and increasingly that competition is no-holds-barred.

Living On Credit

Put it on plastic, the marketers whisper and cajole and exhort. Maxed out? Well, here's two more offers for credit cards in the mail. Just sign here and send it right in! The marketers do not seem to care that some of us won't be able to manage that kind of debt. Many of us will wind up facing bills that are staggering to us, and which may threaten our shelter, our clothing, our food. We may not have been poverty-stricken before, but we are trapped in the debtor's treadmill now. The marketers leave those problems to the back-side of their operation, the merciless telephone collectors and the computer-generated threats of lawsuits. And keep right on pouring out the offers for more credit, more goods. It's your fault if you succumb to all the blandishments, seems to be the corporate viewpoint.

I can't help but wonder what's next.

A resurgence of debtor's prisons? Have we forgotten our history, that many of our original colonists came here fleeing debtor's prison, perhaps as many as sought religious freedom? No doubt the money-lenders of Old England were just as merciless as the corporate collectors of today.

Whether you can afford all this "stuff" they try to sell you or not, you cannot ignore the constant siren allure of the advertising. Nor can your children. Even if you resist the temptation to sink into debt, it can come to seem that no matter what you have, no matter what you do, it isn't enough. Especially the young, not yet trained in critical thinking, can feel impoverished and unworthy because they don't sport known brand names. Speaking of which, where are the classes in our schools to TEACH critical thinking? There is a crying need for such skills.

Why, the sophistication of our advertising these days could make eunuchs rush out to buy Viagra!

If Joseph Goebbels, the Third Reich inventor of the term "big lie" for Adolf Hitler, had access to the Madison Avenue techniques of today, combined with our media technology, I believe the entire world would be goose-stepping. Which by the way makes me wonder just when some man "on a white horse" (or in a beer hall) may learn to apply standard consumer tactics to a bid for rulership of this nation.

Would Americans surrender, say, their right to vote, in return for insured health care?

Don't answer too quickly.

During all the coverage about the young Cuban lad and the battle for his custody between Castro's Cuba and his America-dwelling relatives, an awful lot of callers to my talk show seemed enamored of the Cuban way of doing things. That's pretty scary when you think of it.

War On Poverty

The "War on Poverty" was a grand and wonderful idea created to fight poverty head-on. An American kind of idea, full of idealism and good intentions. Where it fell short was in the execution.

Some fundamental mistakes were made in the war, I think. Remember the adage that when you give a man a fish you feed him today, but when you teach him to fish, you feed him for a lifetime? Some see welfare as giving the poor that fish. Recent efforts aimed at taking those fish away in order to force the recipients to go fishing, so to speak, were an expression of frustration at the intractable nature of people who could not seem to find the will to get off the rolls by themselves.

But as a compassionate society, which I believe we still are, we can't just take away the fish and expect the rest to follow.

We must first make some effort to ensure those being deprived have been taught, and mastered, fishing skills. Beyond that, to carry the analogy to its final step, we must see that there are fishing grounds available to employ those skills.

The great public works projects of the Depression era, almost forgotten today, put an awful lot of people to work, put a lot of money in circulation, and boosted the overall economy to boot.

If the much-vaunted private sector keeps insisting on a corporate right to move whole industries off shore and into foreign low-wage areas, the worst of which are sweat shops, perhaps it's time for them to share the windfall profits of such decisions. The U.S. government could impose taxes on those companies in proportion to their new profit margins, higher taxes where identifiable sweatshops are employed, and use this money for Depression style public employment. If America's free enterprise is going to forsake its workforce, it's time for Uncle Sam once more to step to the plate.

There are thousands of people on the welfare rolls who want to work, ache to work, but their subsistence safety net actually provides for them better than the low-wage dead-end jobs for which they might qualify.

Every time an attempt is made to raise the minimum wage, the corporate money interests wage unremitting war against it in the halls of Congress. They assert that such "inflation" will drive businesses under. They unfailingly threaten to take more jobs offshore.

Yet many of the states which have passed a higher minimum wage than the federal standard have not suffered in terms of any reduction in employment. In fact, according to a report by the National Economic Council in March 2000, studies show that a higher level of wages can actually encourage motivation, retention and an employer's ability to attract skilled workers. This challenges the conventional wisdom that employers would respond by cutting the number of employees.

Nutrition and health care are fundamental. Some mechanism must be found to provide a clear path for these to people trying to fight their way off welfare.

It's hard to convince a single mother that her children will be better off if she goes to work with no health insurance coverage, at a wage that makes purchasing her own impossible, when health care is available to her children as part of the welfare safety net.

We have to learn how to humanely balance the societal safety net to protect our less privileged citizens, and at the same time prod as many of them as we can into productive lives. Part of that responsibility is teaching them how to produce, and the other part is providing an opportunity for them to produce.

Poor and Too Many Kids

Speaking of production, the problems are complicated by impoverished families with multiple kids. Some couples, particularly younger ones, seem to "produce" kids with no thought of how they will afford the care they require. The problem that we as a compassionate society face is that the children are there, they're alive, and any harsh measures against the parents will penalize the innocent young.

I suppose it would take a form of Utopia before people will stop having kids until they can afford to raise them.

Just for thinking purposes, consider a technological Utopia.

In this society, young people of the underclass who reach child-bearing age would be required by law to deposit their eggs or sperm in a government-run bank. They would then be sterilized.

In order to raise a family from their own DNA, they would be required to demonstrate financial responsibility. Once they qualified, they could make withdrawals from their "account" for each child they could afford.

I know this is a pretty scary "Big Brother-ish" scenario.

But I find the specter of children sprouting like weeds in the decaying cores of our inner cities just as scary. These environments are toxic, offering slim to no hope for improvement in their lives. As they reach teen years (or even earlier) far too many of these turn to crime. Each time a generation of the hopeless reaches its hormonal years, crime rates climb.

I noticed one seldom-cited study while working on this book. It compared abortion rates since legalization, and projected those numbers forward to where—absent abortion—the unwanted children would have been in the violent young years. A correlation was found between decreased crime rates and the non-presence of the aborted children.

This study was too cold-blooded for many. But it surely gives food for thought. Is society required to tolerate the helter-skelter birthing of children to anyone who reaches puberty? If so, the poverty-crime cycle seems unlikely to ever be broken.

So what do we do? Let the undisciplined procreation continue, and then yank the kids out of the most irresponsible families and relocate them to families or group homes who can and will raise them well?

That sounds as Big Brother-ish as my technological Utopia, doesn't it?

But these issues must be somehow addressed, or we will continue to live with things like second graders filching a revolver from their crack-besotted adult chaperon and taking it to school. That's an extreme case, but the streets of our inner cities are crowded with dead-end kids with little hope of a future, and no adult role models worth the name. Who's to say what's around the corner next in terms of violence and children?

Juvenile Delinquency Areas

Sadly, none of this is a very new problem in America. A book published in 1929 by a man named Howard Shaw entitled *Delinquency Areas* concluded that certain poor neighborhoods in Chicago always led in juvenile delinquency, regardless of the ethnic mix. Then, between the beginning of World War Two and the end of President Johnson's term, over four million black Americans migrated from the rural South to the big cities of the North. Overcrowding reached epidemic proportions, schools went to double shifts, and urban poverty replaced rural poverty for many of the migrants. Hard drugs appeared on the scene, and crime began to rise.

At the same time, manufacturing employment from the "smokestack" industries which had drawn the migration in hopes of jobs and a secure future, began to decline. New York, Chicago, Detroit, Pittsburgh and other major cities had fewer jobs to offer. Welfare rolls began to climb. Amid the teeming underemployed and unemployed, a community bitterness began to simmer that eventually erupted in the riots of the 60s.

Sociologists of the period advanced a new twist on juvenile delinquency that squares with my concept of manufactured pain. They found that teenage males experienced serious emotional turmoil when what they wanted—all the advertised goodies of the postwar boom years—contrasted so heavily with what they could have in their impoverished circumstances. Delinquency—the word in vogue then for crime by adolescents—became an alternative method for attaining status and achieving success for those denied the middle-class kind of success.

Some would say this is an apologist's approach. That the individual is ultimately responsible for his own social deviancy. I tend toward thinking that way myself—but the fact remains that if there is no avenue of escape from despair, the human species will invent one. Social costs to us all from the despair-generated crime of our ghettos are enormous. And society must share some of the burden for creating those costs; we still don't seem to have learned that in addition to teaching a man how to fish, we must provide fruitful fishing grounds.

Community Based Boards

That said—and contrary to some opinions that the Great Society's War on Poverty was a major defeat—a study of the literature will reveal that during the War, the percentage of Americans classified as poor decreased, with black Americans recording the most significant increases. Thousands of inner-city dwellers migrated once more, out away from the crime-ridden central cores.

Those who stayed behind—those who either couldn't or wouldn't participate in the various programs—were victimized by steadily rising rates of unemployment, illegitimacy, crime and the physical deterioration of the neighborhoods. The ghettos had been dying all along, and in hindsight, the War on Poverty was fighting against the tide when it attempted to create opportunities in the ghettos. Where federal programs opened up jobs and housing that enabled the continued escape from urban blight, a good number of successes were scored.

Without going into the whole political history, there was a good deal of political infighting behind the scenes over which agencies would manage federal programs, and how. In the end, a model of community based boards, comprised of local residents, was chosen. It was sort of like the school board model, of which I've spoken elsewhere. The theory appeared to be that the target community knew what was best for it. Sometimes it worked just that way, just as sometimes school boards manage effective school districts. But with diverse groups of people possessing no real management skills doling out the federal grants locally, waste and even corruption dogged a number of such programs.

Congress then, and Congress now, seems to have an institutional antipathy to the idea of an American welfare state. During the Cold War, with Communist influence seen or suspected everywhere, any idea smacking of a redistribution of wealth was suspect. The mixed results of the community action groups did nothing to alleviate that hostility.

Decline in Poverty?

In late 1999, the White House announced that poverty rates are declining in this country, perhaps as a result of the robust economy.

But that's hardly a signal to sit back. The size of the problem is still enormous, and it still affects all our lives. When you can drive through an impoverished neighborhood—and there are many in this land—and feel the latent frustration and hostility simmering, a statistical drop doesn't seem that encouraging.

Federal intervention of any sort in issues of poverty didn't even begin until early in the twentieth century. Until then, "charity begins at home" was the motto and "poor house" was more than just a term. Families, churches and communities were expected to care for the less fortunate. Church people were the first to see that more was needed, and ministers recruited the newspaper barons of the time to their cause. With churches and the influential newspapers pushing it, government backed welfare, particularly for children, became a reality in the early 1920s.

Then came the Great Depression, and unemployment rates of 25 percent, and "the dole."

By the 1950s, riding the wave of postwar prosperity, there was what has been described as a surge of resentment from wage earners against those receiving "entitlements." But the discourse created by this put poverty on the table again as a national issue, and social welfare experts at one point in the early 1960s concluded poverty could be all but eliminated by federal expenditures of $2 billion a year.

The time was ripe for President Johnson to seize the initiative and proclaim his War on Poverty in his 1964 State of the Union address.

Congress that year appropriated half of what the experts had said would be needed for the first year of the war. The amount was nearly doubled the next session, and increased in succeeding years, if not so dramatically.

But the war faltered with political infighting. Members of Congress didn't like the federal grants coming into their districts outside of their control. They missed publicity opportunities by announcing and appearing to control the grants. Governors and mayors too resented the community action superstructure that was outside traditional political chains of command.

Almost everyone agrees now that Johnson's war was ultimately lost; poverty is still here, and it is still tragic and alarming. Liberals say Johnson was distracted by his other war, Vietnam. Conservatives say the government simply isn't built to conduct such a campaign.

Whatever the reasons, poverty remains.

And it will take a re-dedication by us all to the concept of a compassionate society, which cares about those who fall through the cracks enough to take strong and consistent action, to ever have a lasting effect on the problem.

Poor Forever?

Will the poor always be with us?

Perhaps. But being poor need not be a disgraceful and debilitating state of affairs or an end unto itself. We owe it to ourselves as Americans to begin working to ensure that it is not. To find ways to provide training, education, opportunity for those so far left behind. I'm a simple observer of events; I don't pretend to have the answers. But I do know we cannot afford a significant percentage of our population to be locked in futility and hopelessness, the breeding ground of more futility and hopeless for succeeding generations.

Pay now, or pay later, in the form of rising crime rates and violence.

CHAPTER 9

Politics

WHILE WORKING ON THIS BOOK, ONE OF MY EDITORS ASKED AN INTEREST-ING QUESTION ABOUT POLITICS: is there a difference between campaign reform and campaign finance reform? After giving the matter some thought, I'm not sure there is. Or if there is, campaign finance reform is the 900-pound gorilla that is so hard to ignore that anything else will have to wait its turn. It has become more and more clear to me that what appears to be at the core of many of this nation's troubles is the worship of money. A casual observer of our contemporary culture might conclude that everything is for sale, and that the meaning of America is an untrammeled market economy.

Our political process today is far more a marketplace in the contemporary sense of value for money received than a marketplace of ideas. What really bothers me is that the proponents of free spending cloak their purchase of power and influence under the auspices of freedom of speech. That is, that corporations and labor unions and associations and political action committees are exercising their First Amendment rights of freedom of expression—with their checkbooks.

To regulate and restrict such expenditures, the argument runs, is to trample on First Amendment principles.

This is balderdash, pure and simple. The framers of our Constitution were properly concerned about balancing majority rule and protection of minority rights, and how to balance effective government with limited intrusion upon individual rights. All the basic tenets of political democracy exist in a dynamic tension with each other. The taxation of private income to create a public treasury is one example. When police powers are exercised in the name of public order, individual rights are at risk. The purpose of Congress and the courts is to balance these tensions.

Vast sums of unregulated and often unreported money, poured into the political procession on behalf of special interests, creates an imbalance that threatens the entire process. Money in this market-mad world is power. Lord Acton's admonition applies here: power corrupts, and absolute power corrupts absolutely.

In today's political arena, the ability to raise funds has become the defining quality of a viable candidate for high office. I have seen figures that suggest that in races for the U.S. House, the candidate who raised the biggest war chest won 92 percent of the time. For the Senate it was 88 percent of the time. Of incumbent members of Congress as of mid-2000, exactly 26 had been outspent by their opponents in their last election—12 senators and 14 house members—16 democrats and 10 republicans. That's under 5% of the 535 members of Congress, and some of them were challenging incumbents. The Almighty Dollar is the real power today in our political arena. Politicians spending more and more time in pursuit of the dollar have correspondingly less time for the concerns of ordinary voters.

Across our nation, voters may not quite understand all the ins and outs of how the money tree is harvested—but they darned sure realize that it is being harvested. A sense of futility and disenfranchisement is the result. Why get involved, why vote even, when the decisions are foreordained by the checkbooks of the powerful?

I submit that this voter malaise bodes ill for the continued health of our nation.

Issue Advocacy

One of the ways that enormous, mind-boggling amounts of money are used to influence our political process is through so-called "issue advocacy." Supposedly, issue advocacy focuses on a specific concern put forward by the advocating group, without concern for who may or may not be running for election. If you can disguise your attempt to unseat a politician behind an issue campaign, then you can freely spend an unlimited amount of money.

The U.S. Supreme Court issued an opinion differentiating "express advocacy" of an issue from campaigning. In a footnote to the ruling, certain "magic words" were excluded from issue advocacy. Some of these included "vote for" and "defeat" and "cast your ballot."

As you shall see, applying the "magic word" test to issue advocacy left a hole big enough to drop our nation through. Alaska included.

Federal law has banned corporate spending on campaigns since 1907, and by labor unions since 1947. But in the 1996 campaigns, estimates I have seen indicate that "issue advocacy" spending ranged from $135 to $150 million.

To the average television watcher, an "advocacy" spot is indistinguishable from a political ad. But they are different. For one thing, the "advocates" face no upper limit on how much they can spend. For another, they are beyond the reach of voters and cannot be held accountable for anything they say.

Yet the Supreme Court has recognized that corporations should not, through the special advantages of their amassed wealth, be able to convert their cash into political war chests with which to incur political debts from elected officials. The Court also has held that disclosure of the origins of political money is a bedrock principle in avoiding corruption or the appearance of corruption.

All well and good. But the "soft money" from "advocates" escapes this scrutiny even when the "issues" seem clearly aimed at specific politicians.

One example: A private "advocacy" group fielded a campaign naming a serving politician. Said he preached family values, but took a swing at his wife. Said his explanation was he only slapped her, but her nose was broken.

Nowhere was there a suggestion to vote him out. Did there have to be?

The AFL-CIO, the association of labor unions, spent $35 million in 1996—all in 44 congressional districts held by Republicans. Not a dollar counted against regulated Democratic expenditures in those districts.

But if they spent all that loot without the intention of unseating Republicans in favor of Democrats, I will pin a tail on your donkey.

The Chamber of Commerce countered with The Coalition, an association of over thirty business groups, to protect "pro-business" Congressmen.

Where in this clash of titans was the voice of the ordinary voter to be heard?

The "Dirty Dozen"

The League of Conservation Voters aired 10,000 spots against twelve Congressmen they called the "dirty dozen." The ads named the congressmen and linked them with alleged anti-environmental positions. They ran during the pre-election period. No one could mistake that the "issue" being advocated was to throw the rascals out. But every penny spent was over and beyond the regulated spending of those vying for the seats.

In a nation of laws and not of men (and certainly not of corporations) as ours was designed to be, representative democracy, in which individuals are elected from the citizenry, is the mechanism by which we govern ourselves. These representatives are often referred to generically as "lawmakers," and, with less respect, as "politicians." I'm not sure when the word politician became either a joke, or epithet, or both, but it's a sad commentary on the state of our particular body politic that this is so.

Well, I've been around politicians in our nation's capital for a long time, and I have some observations on them as a group which may not set well with your preconceptions.

It is my considered opinion that politicians who obtain high public office are, as a group, smarter, harder-working, more ethical and more concerned about the future of our nation than—well, than any of the rest of us.

Anyone who believes otherwise has succumbed to what I call pseudo-populist nonsense. Politicians are men and women who truly do see the world as it is, have some strong ideas of how it ought to be, and set out dedicated to making a difference.

Even the ones who turn corrupt began as idealists.

As Ernest Hemingway said about romantic liaisons, "All true wickedness begins in innocence."

In politics in this nation today, unfortunately the romance is with the Almighty Buck, as I described above.

How does the romance with Big Money begin?

Making of a Politician

For many years, I have watched with sadness the deterioration of ideals under the wear and tear of re-election demands. I can predict the conversation now when I interview a politician about his or her views on how the dollar came to rule almost their every move.

The sad processional goes like this: You are an idealist; you want to make a difference. You find the issue or issues that you urgently believe need addressing. You find like-minded people. You exuberate in the freedom of this nation, in that your band of Davids can take on the existing Goliaths of incumbency, win or lose. Maybe you lose a time or two, getting your sea legs. But you learn. And one day the voters have had enough of the "rascals" in power and sweep you in. It's your turn!

Say you are now a member of the U.S. House of Representatives. You're like Jimmy Stewart; you're Mr. Smith going to Washington.

Then you actually get there, and reality sets in.

There are agendas within agendas, issues, party-line votes, special pleaders. You're mighty lucky to get any kind of attention to the issues on which you campaigned at all. Meanwhile the folks at home are confidently expecting miracles. You dig in with a zest; you will learn this Byzantine system better than anybody, play the game, develop your strategy, find your feet.

You look up, and a year has passed.

The hometown media is asking if you're going to run for re-election. Hopefuls back home are testing the waters with some pretty sharp remarks about your so-far ineffectiveness, real or imagined. If you're going to get your agenda on the table, you need allies. If you're going to get another two years to pursue some of the alliances you are developing, you have to run again.

If you're going to run again, you need money.

Lots of money.

PACs

Enter the Political Action Committees (PACs) whose smooth talking representatives for this or that special interest say they have noted your good work, admire you, and want to help. And oh, by the way, relax a little; incumbents have a lot better shot at coming back than those newbies do. We can develop some "issues" advertising that will sink them in the primary. Won't even be traceable to you. We don't think they're the kind of folks we want representing the district back here. You are! You're the right stuff.

And maybe along comes a senior pol from your side of the aisle to inform you about his "leadership" PAC. Any Congressman or Senator can receive $1,000 per primary and per election from any source. In addition, if they create a "leadership PAC" that separate organization can receive $5,000 a year from any source. Organizations with big money can cough up $10,000 to the leadership PAC every two years of a Congressman's term. For Senators, it's $30,000 over a six-year term.

The only apparent catch is that the "leader" cannot spend this "leadership" money on his or her own campaign.

However...

There is nothing to keep them from spending it on your campaign.

Why should such a leader want to bestow this largess on one of the most junior of members? Well, because within the House, or the Senate, each representative still gets one full vote. And it takes votes to obtain key leadership positions on crucial committees.

The PACs supply the leadership money. The anointed "leader" bestows much-needed cash on your re-election effort. The quid pro quo is that you vote for him when committee memberships are on the table—and he will be seeking those committee positions of most interest to the PACs which supplied his leadership treasury.

Nifty how it works, isn't it?

There is ample evidence that this is how influence and key posts are purchased within Congress; representatives struggling with campaign finance, and who are helped out by the older dogs, are very likely to cast their vote the right direction for those important committees.

After a cycle or two of this market-driven cynicism, the politician who has been sucked into the exchange will explain it all to me (and

I've heard this scores of times) based on a solid rationalization.

The rationalization goes like this:

"I have important work to accomplish here. I need to be here to see it's carried on. The only way I can get back here is to play ball with the fundraisers and fund sources. It's not that I love associating with these people, or love this method of getting my work done. But there is no other way. I wish there was another way."

Campaign Finance Reform—Not Any Time Soon

Campaign finance reform, however, seldom seems very popular with those who have adapted to the way it is now. No one seems to want to be the first to rock the boat. There are exceptions, and they are almost universally regarded as quixotic. Or pinko.

While there is an element of truth in the rationalizations that politicians offer for maintaining the status quo, they could be freed of those bonds by realistic campaign reform. But I'm betting it won't happen anytime soon, not until the American public has had enough of government by checkbook and stands up on its hind legs.

That will require action by each of us, something that seems in scarce supply. Which is a shame, because we are neglecting our obligation as citizens to demand the cleaning of our political stables.

It's not likely those who are elected into the system and learn to survive it will seriously undertake reform until we prod them heavily. If we remain apathetic, we will deserve what we get: a weakened democracy.

I don't want to sound too alarmist: democracy is not a hothouse flower.

It has survived many campaign-funding scandals, from the corporate greed that Abraham Lincoln predicted would be the ruin of the Republic during the Civil War to Watergate.

But neither is our form of government as sturdy as crabgrass. It needs some attention from its owners—that's us, folks.

If we don't do it—if we are content to focus on our six packs and wide screens and grumble only when Presidential debates supplant our favorite programming—there are others who are quite willing to run this nation for us. Some of them might even believe they are operating in our best interest.

But one thing these people will ensure, for sure, and that is that the county is operating in their own best interest!

The Power Brokers

Many of the power brokers, representing various special interests, truly believe they are better at managing the affairs of this nation than the voters are. They frame the debates, finance the candidates, consult marketing polls to find percentages of citizens who endorse their particular world view. (Benjamin Disraeli, no mean politician in his own right, coined the phrase "lies, damned lies, and statistics".)

Some would argue that's a grand American tradition too, in that even during our nation's founding, "the equestrian class" of educated white male planters assumed the responsibility of doing what was best for America. Against this view, Thomas Jefferson set his egalitarian position of one person, one vote. This debate remains vivid and alive today, though most of us pay scant attention.

I recently counted over 20 telephone book pages worth of associations listed in the Metro D.C. white pages, ranging from cherry blossom associations to an association for studying walls and ceilings. And of course there was an association for associations.

Americans have a passion for associating. The British have been known to joke that when two Americans meet anywhere in the world, they shake hands. When three or more Americans meet, they form an association and elect officers. I would add that when the associations enter the political arena, as almost all of these do, the next step is assessing members for contributions to direct toward key politicians.

The Congress of Industrial Organizations (CIO), a labor federation, circumvented federal law against unions contributing to election campaigns by gathering money independent of dues through its association. John L. Lewis personally delivered a check for $250,000 in 1936 to President Franklin D. Roosevelt. Roosevelt initially refused, but his campaign handlers had second thoughts. By the time the votes were being counted, his campaign had received over half a million dollars from the CIO. Big bucks in 1936!

The U.S. has a 200-year history of privately funded public elections. Even George Washington got in trouble in 1757 when he allegedly purchased a quart and a half of rum, wine, beer or hard cider for each of 391 voters in the House of Burgesses race in which he was embroiled.

From Washington's liquid payola to Roosevelt's union half-million to today's tens of millions is only a matter of degree, when you think about it.

Studies I have seen indicate that 80 percent of campaign financing in recent high-ticket Congressional elections comes from Political Action Committees, the largest percentage of which represent corporate interests, trying to protect their bottom line.

Is it any wonder that "our" representatives have an open door policy to the magicians who produce so much money to keep them in office?

I don't think it is curious at all.

I don't think it is curious that special interest groups make such titanic efforts to buy those open doors on behalf of their clients.

What I do find curious is that the rest of us put up with it.

The dollar-purchased vote is a marketplace type phenomenon. The free market is one part of a free nation. It is not the only, nor should it be, the primary driving force. In politics, in this nation of laws and not of men, one person, one vote should be the rule, irrespective of corporate backing.

This Is Not Free Speech

I for one am tired of hugely-financed political campaigns as slick as Madison Avenue advertising whose only purpose seems to be to deliver the cleverest or most telling salvo of one-liners. I'm tired of campaigns which use dramatic techniques adapted from documentaries (or tabloid journalism) to drag opposing candidates through the mud. I'm tired of the frantic competitiveness, closely allied to big-brand advertising, to keep the viewer from grabbing the TV remote.

I know all this din of campaign rhetoric, coming at us from all sides, is deemed to be "free speech" at its best. (And the money-handlers assert that free spending is also a form of free speech.)

I don't agree.

I think the time has come to consider that true free speech, in which significant ideas are placed before the voters, will require regulation, careful and considered, to level the playing field.

Let me give an example.

When a case is argued before the U.S. Supreme Court, each side has precisely the same amount of time to set out their position. No bells, no whistles, just the unvarnished arguments. The words of the attorneys, and their relevance, are the issue before the court, not "production" values or camera angles.

I would like to see the length of our political campaigns severely curtailed, as is done in England. You have a five-week campaign season, ending on voting day. Period. Such a brief and concentrated period tends to focus the issues more clearly. Couple this with regulation of "soft money" peripheral, such as glossy TV spots purchased by a special interest group not accountable through the campaigner's organization. Eliminate the high price associated with broadcast advertising. The broadcast industry can afford five weeks of true public service time a year. The government has given the industry free access to vast amounts of public airwaves. It's time for them to give some of it back in aid of good government.

For TV, give each candidate a full-face talking head shot and let them persuade the voters they know what they're talking about. For radio, the candidates' voices, not the dulcet tones of trained voice-actors. For print, position papers.

Voters deserve to see cogent arguments presented in a similar fashion from those who would run our country, so we can judge the content of the arguments and not their trappings. We deserve this fully as much as a bank of Supreme Court justices do.

The political parties would be free to do all the internal wrangling and maneuvering they wanted to select their candidate for the campaign. But on opening day of election season, it would be just the candidates, talking to the voters, no suave voice-over, no dramatic music, no sunsets or rocket's red glare. For five weeks—or whichever period we select as appropriate.

Then we vote, and get back to the business of living.

This way, politicians get to spend far more of their time governing than selling themselves to this or that funding source. I think more of them would find the courage to develop their own opinions on vital issues such as schools and defense. They might even stop obsessively perusing the latest polls financed by this or that political action committee. They wouldn't feel obligated, for one thing.

For another, relieved of the need to constantly court the money-bearers, they would have a heck of a lot more time to interact with us, the people who hired them to represent us.

Finally, one of my poems for your consideration.

SPEAK UP, AMERICA!

On a topic, hot
Political campaigns—
what ought and ought not

Be allowed to take place
on radio, TV or in printed space

The Supreme Court has ruled—
some call it rash—
equating free speech with cold hard cash

Special interest groups groups, now so prolific,
pursue agendas quite specific
Seek politicians, cash in hand...
just as our Founding Fathers planned?

Should all of this be the legal norm?
Or should campaign finance be reformed?
Our candidates spend many hours
paying homage to the financial powers

One person one vote has become a distortion
of Big Money's influence, its powerful portion
Well...perhaps I'm voicing a fruitless gripe
but maybe the time is actually ripe

To officially rename ourselves U.S.A. Inc.
T'would be more honest I sometimes think
Then we could, through incorporation,
become a true free-enterprise nation.

To vote anymore, you'd buy a share...
or two...or ten thousand...the buck will stop there,
In the voting booth, depending how much,
you spend for your choices for freedoms and such.

Who cares if self-determination thrives?
Stockholders determine what happens in our lives.
Let's set this new goal and not be shy...
the best government money can buy!

CHAPTER 10

Foreign Policy

THIS BOOK MAKES NO SECRET OF MY LOVE FOR THE UNITED STATES, for the grand ideas of our founding fathers, and my hopes for the future, despite all the problems we face. I have concentrated almost entirely on issues within our borders, but no look at our nation would be complete without some sort of an evaluation of American foreign policy.

Let me state right up front that such a topic is worth a book all of its own, if not a set of volumes.

Americans have had a love-hate relationship with foreign policy for our whole history. Largely, we have tended to believe that anything of importance to us stops at our own borders. This would appear to be an extension of our commonly held belief, espoused by no less than Benjamin Franklin, that "good fences make good neighbors." We'll concentrate on feathering our own nest and let the rest of the world go by, or at least that seems to be the prevailing sentiment.

In its extreme form, this attitude is labeled "isolationism," the idea that America can and should withdraw from the global stage. This creates an unfortunate vacuum, in my view, which often leads to all sorts of unpleasantness that we sooner or later have to deal with. Unfortunately, today, I see us tail-spinning toward a new sense of political isolationism even as economists trumpet the advent of the "global village."

I think that now would be exactly the wrong time in history to indulge in political isolationism. We cannot let the financial interests, as represented by border-spanning mega-corporations, lay the ground rules for global economy. Business alone is poorly suited to Realpolitik. We as Americans must support (even insist upon) a government that is willing to actively get involved across the world. I think this will require pre-emptive intervention in hot spots to settle this old world down and prevent massive abuses of human rights.

American Interests

We hear much about "American interests" during a debate over whether to involve ourselves, our aid, and ultimately our troops, in foreign lands. The concept of "American interests" too often translates into economic benefits, and not into humanitarian and idealistic interests.

I am not against business and trade, and I think business and trade need global stability to function adequately, build wealth and furnish jobs. But I insist that our interests as Americans transcend availability of a particular fossil fuel, harvest of some profitable crop, or economic concerns about some other commodity. Our interests must include a stubborn insistence upon recognition of those ringing ideals forged by our Founding Fathers: that all men (and women) are created with certain inalienable rights, and that among those are life, liberty, and the pursuit of happiness.

We are the unchallenged super-power today. Like the fictional Superman, it is time for us to use our powers only for good. It is not time for us to be ashamed of who we are, and how we came to be, and to be hesitant before tyrants.

Strong words, yes, but I firmly believe in them.

Any discussion of foreign policy is like peeling an onion; the more you consider the issues between nations, the more leaves you peel away. You find yourself examining the whole "core" of history as it were: the rise of nationalism, the mistakes and triumphs of the past, the lessons of history.

I spoke about our history in the education chapter, but I need to touch upon it again here. When I was in school, students were required to study the great events of our own history as well as the magnanimous statesmen, brave generals, ingenious inventors and industrialists who made us great. By the time we reached voting age, and some of us moved into politics and decision-making, we were firmly grounded in our own identity. I think we still have to know who we are before we can interact adequately with the world around us.

The State of Our History

It is deeply troubling to read accounts, then, like one a few years ago by C. B. Thompson, an American history professor at Ashland University in Ohio, with five years of study of his own in an Ivy League school and years of conferences for professional historians under his belt. Thompson asserted in an essay for the John M. Ashbrook Center for Public Affairs that American history has been "covertly hijacked" by left-wing academics. He says that our junior and high school students today are being taught that the settling of North America represents the single greatest act of genocide in human history; that our Founding Fathers were racist, sexist, classist, homophobic, phallo-centric, Euro-centric bigots.

Thompson goes on to say that the new National Standards for United States History, sanctioned by our government and paid for by our tax dollars, will barely mention George Washington, our Constitution or Lincoln's Gettysburg Address. Instead they'll focus on things like the first nineteenth century assembly of feminists and the rise of the American Federation of Labor—most worthwhile activities, and ones long overlooked, but hardly the whole or even dominant story of our national growth. Much more emphasis will be placed on the evils of "robber barons" like John D. Rockefeller and politicians like Joseph McCarthy than on the successes of those like Thomas Edison and the Wright Brothers.

And he said a survey of what American historians think found Karl Marx more popular than Alexis de Tocqueville. *The Autobiography of Malcolm X* was more popular than the Federalist Papers.

What has this to do with our foreign policy? Well, mighty oaks from little acorns grow, as the old saw has it, and our little acorns that will grow to maturity to prosecute our nation's foreign policy are being influenced by teachers who don't think much of our American culture.

This struck a strong chord with me in preparation of this book, because I found myself reading the remarks of Jawaharlal Nehru, an early leader of India after its independence in 1947 from British colonial rule. Nehru spent a lot of time in jail before independence, much of it during the Great Depression. He felt that the Depression was the responsibility of unrestrained capitalism. That was not a terribly unusual view in those days. Marx of course was the chief proponent of it.

In his autobiography, Nehru said:

"...I watched and studied as far as I could in jail, the world situation in the grip of the great depression... India with her problems and struggles became just a part of this mighty world drama, of the great struggle of political and economic forces that was going on everywhere, nationally and internationally. In that struggle my own sympathies went increasingly toward the Communist side... Much in Soviet Russia I dislike—the ruthless suppression of all contrary opinion, the wholesale regimentation, the unnecessary violence (as I thought) in carrying out various policies. But there was no lack of violence and suppression in the capitalist world, and I realized more and more how the very basis and foundation of our acquisitive society and property was violence. Without violence it could not continue for many days. A measure of political liberty meant little indeed when the fear of starvation was always compelling the vast majority of people everywhere to submit to the will of the few, to the greater glory and advantage of the latter..."

Powerful and thoughtful words from the man credited with creating such terms as "Third World," "neutralism," and "non-alignment" as an alternative to taking sides between two clashing titans of Capitalism and Communism. The man who would be leader of the largest democracy in the world, where Communist and Socialist parties routinely had candidates stand for election like other parties.

Capitalism was often seen as the pervasive evil in parts of the world colonialized by the Western nations. The colonial powers grew wealthy on the natural resources of their colonies; to the colonized, that sometimes seemed to be the sole and only objective of the occupation. This despite the fact that some colonizers, most notably the British, taught the rudiments of self-government toward the end of their reign, and even the most repressive colonial powers often built a modern industrial infrastructure in their subjugated lands. Somehow in the grand scheme of things, the United States, first colony to break free and declare (and make stick) its independence, became associated with the colonial masters, instead of being seen as the torch-bearer for others.

While it may be overly simplistic, I think some of the fault for that lies in past isolationist practices of our nation.

The India-Pakistan Fiasco

After World War Two, when the weakened British Empire wanted out of India, it hit upon the idea of partitioning the continent, dividing India and Pakistan into separate nations, largely along religious lines (India largely Hindu and Pakistan predominantly Muslim). India had a long history, rooted in Hinduism, of religious tolerance. Even Muslims were welcome. Muslims, of course, do not reciprocate this tolerance. And as for democracy, that is something their theocratic rulers seem to have a low tolerance for.

The Solomon-like partitioning of India was bloody and violent, and led to a history of tensions and outright wars between the two nations.

India became one of the first nations to recognize Red China diplomatically, largely because the Asian giant shouldered against Pakistan on its other side, and could be a valuable ally. Red China in those days was virtually a client state of the Soviet Union, and the Soviets were happy to funnel supplies and weaponry to a new nation that was unwieldy and poverty stricken and viewed as rich ground for further Communist inroads. Recognition of Red China by India was a thorn in our side, because the United States supported Formosa. In the stress of Cold War policy, the U.S. sided with Pakistan, something still resented in India's halls of power.

So what, you may ask? Pakistan provided a base of operations from which to support the Afghanistan war against the Soviet Union, which is generally credited with sapping the will of the Soviet bear, perhaps being the last straw that broke the back of the "evil empire."

There are no easy answers in foreign policy, though.

Pakistan now is ruled by a "junta" (a council or committee for political or governmental purposes, especially a group of persons controlling a government after a revolutionary seizure of power). Muslim rule is not noted for its human rights record anywhere. Brawling, sprawling, multi-ethnic India and the Muslim Pakistan still face each other at daggers' points—and this time the daggers have the shape of nuclear warheads.

Would history have taken a different course if American foreign policy had been handled differently here? And what of the future? What do we do now?

The China Challenge

Adjoining these quarreling cousins is China, a massive totalitarian state with many troubles of its own, and with no Soviet Union to prop it up any more. Where the Soviet Union attempted to relax political totalitarianism and hang onto economic control, China appears to be trying the other route. They are attempting to open up economic channels to the West while maintaining their iron totalitarian grip.

For now, they seem to be managing, but I suspect it is just a matter of time until Chinese leadership will have to loosen the reins—or risk becoming a backwater to history, losing their status as a world power. Trade will open a lot of eyes. A free exchange of information will give the Chinese people a vision of what can be, what they could have... and they will want some.

American-Chinese Trade

America's role, in my view, will be to show willingness to trade, to invite China to the table. In the meantime, we should make it clear that our continued cooperation is contingent upon Chinese leadership easing up on their hard-line suppression of free expression, assembly, religion—the very things that the United States at our birth set out as the inalienable rights of man.

America's Responsibility to the World

Isolationism on our part is turning our back on the ideals that made our nation great. The ideas that our founders set forth in the Declaration of Independence, and later in our Constitution, have resulted in the longest-standing democracy on earth. America is a vast conglomeration of people from every corner of the globe, every ethnic background, and every religion—where the succession of power takes place peacefully every four years like clockwork.

We are in the world and of the world, and we influence that world by our very existence and history. Today in our country, with all our forms of communication from television to e-mail, we are much closer to our elected representatives than were the scattered farmers and frontiersmen of the eighteenth and nineteenth history. We need to let them know that we are ready and willing for our nation to step in where necessary.

By this I mean assertive diplomacy and, yes, force of arms if required to prevent genocide, massacres, or ethnic cleansing. And I mean we should do it whether or not there is a clear economic incentive ("American interest") at stake. Isolationism lets tyranny fester and grow malignant, and the butcher bill gets higher the longer it goes unchecked. Had Britain and France resisted Hitler's re-arming of the Rhineland, which was in violation of the Versailles Treaty, we now know from Nazi records that Hitler had given orders for his troops to withdraw. How much resolve in the thirties could have minimized the bloodbath of the forties?

Before technology swept us up, the vast ocean bulwarks of the Atlantic and Pacific lent geographic support to isolationism. What transpired beyond the seas had little to do with us. Wars and rumors of wars in far-off lands were just stories in the newspapers.

But throughout the entire twentieth century, the evidence has been strong that that view is out of date. We opted out of the first World War for a long time, and the European nations locked in a bloodletting that seemed interminable—until a slogan was coined that appealed to the American spirit: "the war to end all wars." The Germans were virtually at the gates of Paris when American doughboys threw their shoulders and their riflery skills into the fray. Our armed men, our idealism, and our industrial clout brought to an end the long, horrid years of bloodbath.

As good as our fighting men and our intentions were, though, our diplomats left something to be desired in sophistication. We let the victors lay down the punitive Versailles treaty. This is not the place to go into all the ramifications that grew out of Versailles. Suffice it to say that without it, Adolf Hitler would have had a harder time finding a crushed and dispirited people ripe for his rants on racial superiority and hate. The whole world reaped the whirlwind of his sowing.

And we, the reluctant giant, again were drawn into the fray. We wound up fighting savage wars across both our oceanfronts, against Hitler in the Atlantic and against the Imperial Japanese in the Pacific.

America — The World's Ineffective Referee

At the conclusion of World War Two, the United States was—as it is again now—the undisputed superpower on this planet. The atomic secrets had not yet been stolen by the Russians; the Chinese Communists were barely emerging from their Long March.

America followed its own best and brightest ideals in the ordering of the peace after this war. The Marshall Plan rebuilt Europe. NATO erected an umbrella of defense against the growing Soviet threat; an umbrella that proved impermeable until the "evil empire" collapsed of its own weight. And in Japan, under MacArthur, our erstwhile foes learned about democracy and free enterprise.

European nations that entered the twentieth century in the uneasy "balance of power" that led to World War One entered the twenty-first century as an economic union, sharing currency and culture and essentially open borders. Warlord-ridden Japan at the beginning of the last century became Japan the world power at the beginning of this one. That didn't happen by accident. It all had its roots in the generosity of the United States in victory.

From that peak of a compassionate foreign policy initiative, the Cold War years seemed to bring reverse after reverse. The United States was in a global death struggle with a relentless foe with an unabashed goal of world dominion. Capitalism had become the secular Satan and America its handmaiden. The Soviets were developing "client states" around the world, igniting unrest and uprisings, claiming more and more real estate for the Hammer and Sickle, making strides in nations like India, as mentioned above.

All this hostile activity warped American foreign policy, like a compass needle reacting to nearby metal, away from its true course. Brutal right-wing regimes around the world began to find that they could get away with any kind of human rights violations against their own people, so long as they were "hard on Communism." That was the "open sesame" for American largesse. Should American diplomats lodge the mildest form of protest against such abuses, the bullies would be quick to threaten rapprochement with the Reds.

Such threats were empty and should not have been given a moment's consideration.

The Soviet Union had no record of intelligent administration to match that of the Roman Empire, which would depose local chieftains and then hand them back their thrones—as agents of Rome. No, the right-wing hard cases would have been the first against the wall if the Soviets moved in.

Our proper response to such threats should have been to play a little hard ball ourselves. Furtherance of human rights is almost inevitably in the long-term best interests of all concerned—except that of the petty tyrants.

We tolerated a tyrant like Batista in Cuba.

And we got Castro as a result.

Anyone with a shred of common sense or foresight could have predicted such a result. When people are pushed—they push back.

We tolerated Somoza…and the backlash gave us Ortega.

These two failures, right in our own hemispheric back yard, demonstrate how our foreign policy had somehow gone badly astray.

Corporate Influence in World Affairs

You may have noted by now that one of my pet peeves is the megabucks corporation with both eyes fixed on its next quarter's profits—and nothing else. Well, when you look behind the scenes at how American foreign policy has seemed shortsighted in the past—contrary to our nation's expressed ideals—it is my opinion that there you will find corporate influence again.

American corporations were so invested in a single year's harvest of a particular foodstuff, mineral or commodity that any expedient would be espoused by their political lobbying arm as a necessary measure to get that profit in.

Come to think of it, such shortsighted profiteering led to the Wall Street crash and the Great Depression. The soup lines and shuttered banks that Marxists identified with all capitalism, and which led to the erroneous conclusion that all free enterprise was evil (kind of like throwing out the baby with the bath water), also led to us propping up regimes not worthy of our support. We sent the gunboats for the wrong reasons, not to fight tyranny, but to protect profits.

Vietnam: The Righteous War

One of the least-understood foreign policy debacles in American history, from my point of view, is the Vietnam War.

I say it was a righteous war, a war against tyranny.

It was a war we could have won, and it was a war we should have won, as I wrote in a recent article for *American Legion Magazine*. Given the mindset of our American history professors, as set out above, there are few more heretical positions that I could take. Over and over during this past quarter century, we have been bombarded by the view that our effort in Vietnam was immoral, illegal and doomed to failure. The conflict hung over American foreign policy like a dark cloud until Operation Desert Storm cleared the political air and established this nation as a superpower worthy of the name again.

Before I get into my thoughts of the war specifically, I would like to point out, again, that a form of isolationism—even in the midst of the Marshal Plan and the rebuilding of Japan—helped set the stage for Vietnam. At the end of World War Two, there was a strong desire among colonies all over the world for independence and independence now. French Indochina was just such a situation. They had fought and died beside the French against the Japanese invaders. They wanted self-determination.

It can be argued, and persuasively, that as a former enclave of colonies ourselves, we should have supported that view and pushed France to free its colony immediately after the war.

Ironically, when our bunch of ragtag colonists declared themselves a free nation dedicated to "life, liberty and the pursuit of happiness," France had been one of the first countries to recognize the upstart United States of America. France had set the historical precedent for the United States to say, "Pardonnez moi, M'sieurs, but turnabout is fair play." And it would have been the right thing to do.

But we didn't do it. The French were driven out by force of arms and the nation divided up into North and South. The North was ruled by Ho Chi Minh and his Communist cadre, and they immediately set out to grab the South, too. The South didn't want to be grabbed, and the U.S. didn't want the Communists to grab it either. We were invited in to defend the new nation. Our involvement in that war had a solid moral underpinning, a basis in international law, and it remained winnable up until the moment of U.S. military withdrawal.

The Truth About Ho Chi Minh

A principal myth surrounding Vietnam is that Ho Chi Minh, the North Vietnamese leader, was some benign nationalist with only a hint of agrarian reformist tendencies, and that he could easily have been converted to a pro-western point of view if the United States had just made the right overtures.

History shows that's just nonsense. In the 1920s, Minh was a founding member of the Communist Party in France. He spent the 1930s in the Soviet Union, backing every murderous purge by Josef Stalin. Later, he joined the Chinese Communist Party, and there forged the links that would facilitate the military supplies he used against the French, against us, and against his own people.

Remember the boat people? They fled the advent of Minh's rule in the South after the fall of Saigon. Remember also that before those two million fled Hanoi's rule, a million had fled North Vietnam for the South in the 1950s. Minh was about as popular as Imperial Japan.

From terror campaigns and purges to mass executions, Ho Chi Minh's regime was a junior version of the Kremlin's, and by conscious design. His life was devoted to despotism, and there is no evidence that we missed an opportunity for turning him into a benign democratic nationalist.

This was not a case of imperialist Uncle Sam placing his boot across the backs of proletarians struggling in revolution. Besides sounding like a script from the Kremlin, it was also completely untrue. The average South Vietnamese was apolitical, but still flocked to the polls during rare voting opportunities despite Communist threats. This pattern has been repeated across the world wherever an authentic opportunity to vote presents itself. The lure of casting a ballot for self-determination is a powerful one and appears to be universal.

South Vietnamese governments were not models of democracy by western standards, but compared with much of the world, their standard of authoritarianism was fairly normal—modeled, in fact, upon the French in many ways. Compared with the butchers of Hanoi, the Saigon regimes would have won the Nobel Peace Prize.

Most importantly for us, the war was a battlefront against organized tyranny. Those who decry the notion of an international Communist conspiracy should note that people are judged by their words and deeds alone. The Communists conspired to rule the world. Have we forgotten Premier Khruschev's threat to "bury" us? Have we forgotten his timetable for putting a Red star on the White House by 1980?

The Soviet Involvement

The "evil empire" came a lot closer than we'd like to think. There was certainly no inevitability to its demise in the 1960s.

There are reasons why the Vietnam War should have been pursued to a successful conclusion. By any measure, available resources of the United States were overwhelmingly superior to those of Hanoi. The Soviets, as with North Korea a dozen years earlier, sent equipment, advisors and whole surface-to-air anti-aircraft missile crews to North Vietnam. They supplied pilots to fly North Vietnamese aircraft. But American pilots still maintained a considerable edge in the skies, and the Soviets were never willing to turn this into a land war between major powers in the face of all the nuclear implications.

Although the Soviets may have wanted to prop up the Hanoi regime, the fact is that the United States was there on the ground first, by invitation, and any insertion of Soviet ground troops would have made them the aggressors. China contributed supplies and advisors, but the People's Liberation Army had yet to recover from the mauling it took in Korea. There's no indication Beijing was willing to risk further huge losses in personnel and equipment, which would have been the cost for full-scale involvement in Indochina.

The North Vietnamese themselves proved tenacious and resourceful, but there is no record of any clash larger than battalion size won by their forces. Any time they went beyond hit-and-run guerrilla tactics, as in Khe Sanh, they suffered terrible and inevitable defeat. The Communists faced an enemy with total air superiority and unprecedented airmobile capabilities. And one of the little-known facts of the war is that our citizen-soldiers were some of the most effective fighting men we have ever fielded, even though the annual rotation made for a persistent supply of inexperienced troops. That was more than balanced by the knowledge that this was, for the most part, a 365-day experience. We had the short-timer calendars to prove it. Imagine the Communist foot soldier, doomed to face American firepower for the duration or death, whichever came first.

The Tet Offensive

The Tet Offensive of 1968 has been cussed and discussed. It was at that time that the man widely regarded as the most trusted voice in America, Walter Cronkite of CBS-TV, began to publicly question our ability to win in Vietnam. President Johnson himself took note of this, saying that if he'd lost Cronkite, he'd lost Middle America. But what really happened during Tet?

Certainly it was a dramatic period of both the war and Communist confidence that bordered on swagger. Coinciding with the Vietnamese New Year's observance, Communist forces tried to occupy nearly every provincial capital as well as portions of Saigon itself. At various times, except for the northern city of Hue, they briefly managed to seize and hold some territory, but only at the cost of their Viet Cong auxiliaries. The VC—the South's so-called indigenous forces—never again contributed units of any significance to the fight.

From that point on, the war in the South was totally waged by North Vietnamese Army regulars, trashing even the notion of some popular uprising among the people of the South.

Tet was a huge gamble, and General Giap rolled snake eyes.

Except, of course, in the eyes of the American public, which was fed a completely distorted picture of what took place. But don't let that misconception alter the historical truth of Tet: it was one of our most dominating, one-sided victories in U.S. history.

How We Could Have Won in Vietnam

The U.S. could have done any number of things in prosecuting the war. We could have occupied a line from the demilitarized zone to the Thai border, cutting off the Ho Chi Minh Trail completely. We could have extended bombing in the North to the dikes, the backbone of North Vietnamese agriculture. And we could have ended, early on, the Communist impunity. Those who say we had no basis for attacking "neutral" nations should remember that neutrality has responsibilities as well as rights. Both Cambodia and Laos, by their acquiescence to the presence of North Vietnamese troops and whole base camps, forfeited any right to be treated as neutral. To those who say neither country had the power to eject Hanoi's forces, I say they could simply have asked for help in restoring the sovereignty of their territory.

Why, in the face of this evidence, do the views persist that the United States fought an immoral war in Vietnam, a war they say never could have been won? Largely because an entire generation has a great stake in maintaining this view. The baby boomers are seen, and see themselves, as people who fought two great battles in the 1960s: for civil rights at home and against the war in Vietnam. Perhaps it was necessary to develop some identity in the face of parents who could merely point to saving the world from a crippling depression and fanatic fascism as their great accomplishments.

For whatever reasons, the boomers identify with the civil rights and the anti-war causes, even those who never marched a step in protest. Therein lies a tragic irony.

The fight for civil rights was among the most noble in history. The irony is that at the same time civil rights demonstrators were bravely demanding the right to vote, the right to peacefully assemble, and the right to speak freely at home for all Americans, others were marching to ensure that the Vietnamese would never have these same rights. That was a tragic betrayal of all that is supposed to make this country great, and a terrible misapplication of our national foreign policy.

The Challenge of Foreign Policy Today

Foreign policy is never as simple as it sounds. But I do believe that the United States needs to develop a strong sense of mission as to its role in the world. If we have to spend time as the world's policeman, so be it.

Alone among all nations in history, when we have held the dominant upper hand, we have not required any kissing of hems or paying of tribute.

We just want a fair price for our goods, and to see some peace and safety for the common man and woman of the world. An opportunity for life, liberty and the pursuit of happiness—for us and for everyone.

We, the American people, have the best chance that any people have ever had to bring that vision true.

But not if we abdicate our role, revise our view of ourselves until we feel like we need to apologize for existing, and crawl back behind our oceans until the next worldwide crisis blows up in our face.

CHAPTER 11

Crime and Punishment

IN RECENT YEARS, NO SUBJECT I CAN THINK OF has taken up more of the public's attention than that of crime and punishment, or lack thereof.

Crime statistics go up, they go down, they stay static, depending on the year and possibly who's compiling the statistics. We in the media fan the flames of concern high with our preoccupation with violent crime.

If you personally have been the victim of a crime, the statistics don't really have much meaning. What you want is some justice for your violated sense of self and safety.

I know there is a whole body of thought that considers retribution for criminal behavior to be more revenge than justice. To me, this is just semantics.

I'll go even further: revenge, properly administered by our system of laws and justice, is a perfectly proper response against criminal behavior.

A criminal assault against a person or persons, or the forcible theft of goods or money, disturbs the natural balance of things. There needs to be an equal and opposite reaction against the one who disturbs the balance.

A large proportion of our citizenry seem to have given up on the notion of "rehabilitation" for convicted criminals. They did the crime, now make them do the time. I agree. The "three strikes and out" legislation that has come to fruition in recent years places the onus squarely on the evil-doer. If two convictions, journeys through the prisons system and freedom again haven't changed his ways, they're unlikely to change.

Third time's a charm for society—and strike three for him. Throw away the key.

So much of serious crime is committed by recidivists, which is a fancy name for people who don't know when to stop. Recidivism takes a nosedive when the unrepentant are locked away for keeps. They're off our streets, out of our homes, away from our loved ones. And good riddance.

The same goes for the death penalty.

I have yet to hear of a multiple murderer, convicted and put to death by the state, repeating his offenses from the grave. And in the case of murderers, particularly, I think society's vengeance is properly exacted. Murder really throws societal balance out of plumb, ravages the victim's survivors, spreads terror.

The somber rituals of the death penalty reset the balance, and give victims' survivors some closure. The state, representing we, the people, makes clear through this ritual that some behavior is not to be tolerated.

Do three-strikes and similarly tough sentencing laws, and the death penalty, serve as deterrents to crime? There seem almost as many opinions on that question as there are researchers. So many other factors are stirred into the making of a felon. A high degree of rational thought does not seem to be among these, or perhaps they would chose some less risky form of enterprise than robbing banks or carjacking or sticking up liquor stores. So perhaps they never stop to think it through to the logical consequences before they pull the trigger on some helpless clerk.

Too bad for them, I say.

As far as the death penalty goes, there is a vociferous minority opposed to the government taking of life, no matter how heinous the crimes for which it is prescribed. Among these are the same individuals who throw every roadblock in the path of a speedy execution, postponing the appointed hour for years—and who then argue that administration of the death penalty is too expensive because of all the delays!

Matching the Punishment to the Crime

In my opinion, many more moderate opponents of the death penalty simply do not trust our justice system to find and convict the actual wrongdoer. Not a year goes by that a convict somewhere, serving a protracted sentence, is not released because of exonerating evidence discovered years later. Years after, even with delays, a death penalty would have been carried out.

Americans have a bone-deep repugnance against miscarriage of justice. My answer to that one is for trial judges to be permitted to instruct juries that the death penalty is not an option in situations where some basis for the essential case may be open to question. Juries may of course reject the whole case and find for acquittal.

We have come a long way since someone could be sentenced to the galleys for stealing a loaf of bread. Efforts to ensure that convicts are not subjected to "cruel and unusual" punishment reflect a societal rejection against the excesses of the past.

But this must be said: tens of thousands of criminals are not misunderstood souls who have lost their way; they are predators, pure and simple. Whether they were spanked or not as children, abused or not, society must not be their victim.

Sometimes, seeing the horrors done against innocent victims, I want to ask what's wrong with a little cruel and unusual?

Or, as Gilbert and Sullivan's Mikado proposed with his method all sublime: let the punishment fit the crime.

I don't know if this is apocryphal or not, but an American policeman who worked under contract in a good-sized city in an Arab emirate—where lopping off a hand is still considered a reasonable punishment for thieves—said a chest of gold could be left on the curb without much risk of loss.

In the spring of 2000, a Pakistani judge made international headlines when he sentenced one of history's most prolific serial killers to be executed exactly as he had destroyed over a hundred young men and boys. That is to say, strangled to death with an iron chain, hacked into pieces and dissolved in a vat of acid.

Naturally, the furor from human-rights group was instantaneous and heated.

The case dropped from the headlines, and I suspect the judgment will never be carried out. It would be difficult to find sane men to perform such a grisly act. Being a state executioner by any method is hard enough on the unsung men who perform this chore. But surely the judge's frustration woke a resonance in many. There were no human-rights advocates to intercede with this monster as he went about his bloody business. It sometimes seems the violator has more rights than the victim. Especially in this nation of ours.

Wherefore Art Thou, Justice?

That said, I am hardly an advocate of a police state where all our civil liberties are sacrificed under the rubric of being hard on crime. Our system of justice, supposedly of laws and not of men, still is adminis-tered by men. It is fallible. Wrongful convictions can and do occur. The power already granted the police and prosecutors are enormous and subject to abuse.

Our criminal courts are choked with backlogs, largely because of the so-called war on drugs, as I covered in my chapter on victimless crime. A basic tenet of our laws is that justice delayed is justice denied. Yet defendants caught up in the toils of the system face interminable de-lays before they can get their day in court. Jury trials are strenuously discouraged, and plea-bargaining is almost out of hand. Is plea-bargain-ing justice?

Look at plea-bargaining from either perspective. A dangerous crim-inal who knows the ropes is allowed to plead down from the crime he actually committed in order to clear a space on the court calendar and ensure an easy victory for the prosecutor. An innocent man or woman, confronted with the debilitating expense and wait before they can come to trial, often defended by an underpaid and overworked pubic defender, is pressured to plead to a lesser charge and get on with their life. The prosecutor has another conviction to add to his or her record for when he or she runs for public office with the stance of being tough on crime. The innocent party has a criminal record.

While I was writing this book, one of the latter cases made head-lines. A woman who was a long-time resident alien of the United States translated an international telephone conversation for a family member about certain travel arrangements. It turned out the travelers were ille-gal drug couriers. The working mother was swept up in the arrests and charged right along with the guilty. Her public defender advised her to plead down to a misdemeanor, take probation, and get on with her life.

Later, she went on an overseas trip. Upon returning, the Immigration and Naturalization Service found her conviction in the ubiquitous government computers and locked her up, thousands of miles from her children, preparatory to deporting her as an undesirable. Her daughter had to leave college to look after her minor children. The media tracked down her public defender, who said he had no idea such ramifications could result from the deal he pressed on his client. The INS remained adamant about her incarceration until public pressure became overbearing, and the agency suddenly discovered an exemption which would permit her to return home.

As I say, our system of justice is a fallible system.

It is my opinion that much of the resistance to severe punishment for the guilty is a widespread distrust of those administer it. Unfortunately, much of that distrust has a basis in fact. The police and prosecutors appear to see their jobs as a matter of clearing cases as fast as possible. In such a hurried atmosphere, mistakes multiply.

Appeals: The Good, The Bad & The Ugly

Another gripe I have with our system involves appeals. Again, from two different perspectives. When appeals courts find that trial courts erred and that prosecutions were flawed, and overturn convictions, we are often treated to the spectacle of prosecutors scrambling to bring other charges against the appellant.

The courts have held that someone was wrongfully incarcerated. There is the prospect of the wrongfully convicted party suing those responsible. So the prosecutors go on the offensive to keep the defendant off balance and in retreat.

I have a harsh opinion of this.

Prosecutors who attempt to resist a reversal of conviction by these means should wind up in jail themselves.

Their job is to do what the law allows them to do. They did that in the original prosecution, and they failed. They wrongfully jailed somebody. If the civil courts find their performance negligent, then the taxpayer should recompense the wronged party. That's justice.

On the other extreme of the appeals process falls those interminable ones which are launched by opponents of the death penalty. These are almost never predicated on wrongful conviction; there is usually little question the convicted party committed the crime. The appeals instead are a willful attempt to stall the execution.

Then these same opponents turn around and argue against the death penalty on the grounds that carrying it out is too expensive due to the protracted appeals process!

Where there is any shadow of doubt that murder was done, the death penalty should not be imposed. In an ideal world, where there is any shadow of doubt, the defendant is acquitted, whether the death penalty is an issue or not. Perhaps the most famous case of the late twentieth century played out this way when O.J. Simpson was acquitted. That case became almost a litmus test of opinion in this country.

Lost in all the hoopla of the televised murder trial of a celebrity was the initial behavior of the Los Angeles Police the morning of the murders.

A soon-to-be famous detective scaled the walls of the Simpson family compound with no warrant or discernible probable cause, admitted his companions, and the rest, as they say, is history. The courts let that questionable incursion stand. I suspect that to stop the case right there would have created a furor equal to all the furors that eventually ensued.

And if O.J. Simpson had not been wealthy, he would have been convicted.

Our criminal court system pits attorneys representing the state and the defendant against each other in a brutal arena, much like a prizefight.

If I'm going to be represented in such a battle, I want somebody with the fistic prowess of a Lennox Lewis fighting for me. But I can't afford heavyweight lawyers. Probably neither can you. If you find yourself caught up in the toils of criminal justice, it will ruin you financially. You may wind up with a harried public prosecutor after your finances run out.

What kind of chance would you have against a prosecution team if murder were the charge?

A major underlying problem in our justice system is that "dream teams" such as that assembled by Simpson can only be had by the wealthy. Prosecutors and police of course know this. Remember their perceived mission is to clear cases. They're overworked and they're in a hurry and they above all do not want to look soft on crime. It's as if you're tied to the tracks and the train is running.

I'd like to see some random justice introduced into the system, and see what might happen.

What if there was a lottery for the services of such high powered legal talent as the team who freed Simpson? There are plenty of premiere defense attorneys across this nation. A rotation could be set up among them so that each of them or a team of them took one case out of the lottery pool over a specified period of time. Funded by the government, at something like their going rate.

Then every prosecutor writing up a charge would have to ask: is this the case that will draw the Dream Team?

Against such a standard, I have a hunch that they would be much more careful in their case preparation. Perhaps much more willing to tell the police they didn't have a case. Combined with rules that placed them at risk if they resisted overturned convictions by attempting to rig up other charges post-facto, perhaps it would focus their attention on the worst offenders.

And ordinary citizens who have fallen under suspicion might be less likely to have to plea bargain their way into the role of a convicted criminal when they know in their hearts they are innocent.

Recognizing that all systems of justice are fallible, our nation was founded on the principle that is better for guilty men to walk free than for one innocent man to be convicted. In the general hysteria about crime in general and drugs in particular, we as a nation seem to have lost sight of that noble purpose.

I think we can have it both ways. Due diligence and care for the rights of the accused, respecting our Bill of Rights, even if it means letting the guilty walk free occasionally, while at the same time building solid and airtight cases against the incorrigible.

CHAPTER 12

The Media

IF A TREE FALLS IN THE FOREST WITH NO ONE TO HEAR—IS THERE A SOUND?
— *Unknown*

Witnesses said the flurry of shots sounded like "a cap pistol."

But five people lay dead after the shots were fired, one of them a pregnant woman whose unborn infant was the sixth casualty. The killer turned out to be a disgruntled estranged husband who had cornered his wife among a group of people and just kept shooting.

Sound familiar? Like something you heard on the way home from work yesterday? Or saw on a news flash interrupting your favorite TV program last night? Or read in a banner headline over your morning orange juice a week ago?

Can you remember where in the country it happened, roughly? Northern Tennessee this time? Southern California? Somewhere in Michigan?

Well, no. And it didn't happen last week, either, or last month, or last year. This particular multiple homicide occurred in 1967. What made it so different from those which seem to occur weekly now, and why do I bring it up now, for this discussion on the state of our nation's media?

One thing, and one thing only.

The only extensive news coverage that this multiple-homicide garnered was a story in the weekly newspaper in the small town where it happened. The closest daily newspaper included five paragraphs in its "police blotter" weekend roundup of county violence. The wire services didn't touch it. Nor did the two local TV stations. A couple of local radio stations reported in their "top of the hour" newscasts that the killer was at large, then that he had been caught.

And that was it.

Today such an explosion of violence anywhere in this nation would occasion news flashes on radio and TV, and lots of headlines. TV choppers would hover over the trailer park, while breathless correspondents interrupted our soap operas and ball games. Talk shows and editorial columns would bemoan the violence in our society. Representatives of this or that special-interest group would be tediously quoted yet again with their formula for stopping such incidents. Some of these formulas don't make sense. Some of them are frighteningly draconian—would erode every one of our Bill of Rights to some degree or other—but we are fed a steady diet of them.

News Is The Unusual

Meanwhile, for the rest of us, there is a growing sense of unease, of being unsafe anywhere. I often hear from listeners who seem willing to exchange freedoms they don't really understand for a stronger sense of security against jeopardies they imagine lurk on every corner.

Were those 1967 deaths any less tragic because they were not the grist of the nationwide media industry?

Was our society any less violent 30 years ago because such violent episodes were not considered newsworthy enough for broad consumption?

Is our society more violent now because every such incident is covered and often sensationalized?

I believe the answer to these three questions is no.

Even though I have spent most of my adult life in some variation of the radio news or talk-show business, I think the modern-day preoccupation that the media has shown for violence has blurred the definition of "news" for all of us.

News is the unusual. Sadly, it's not that unusual, and never has been, for some people to blow a gasket and kill other people. On the other hand, it's not as if we live in a constant war zone either.

That blurring has perhaps helped foster a nationwide sense of malaise, of apathy, almost of fatalism. The steady diet of awful news ("If it bleeds—it leads" is the watchword of the day) may satisfy our morbid sense of curiosity about the violent and macabre. In a "market-driven" philosophy of news coverage, the media consultants will advise news directors to give the market what it wants to hear/see/read. (I'll talk about "market-driven" news a bit more later.)

But what happened to the concept of journalistic responsibility? Of reporting things the people need to know, should know, in order to comprise an informed electorate, the keystone of a democracy? What about some sense of balance, let alone propriety?

It was that responsibility that the Founding Fathers had in mind when they crafted the media protections of the First Amendment.

There are programs on the air that would never have been tolerated 30 years ago, or even 20. I don't mean by this that there would have been rules or regulations to prohibit them; I simply mean there would have been such a pressure of disapproval from opinion-shapers and from peers in the business that the programs would never have seen the airwaves.

The line between journalism and entertainment—and between entertainment and programs designed to shock—continues to blur. How far can this trend go before shock ceases to have any value? I'm afraid to project in this area, because as soon as the public seems to become inured to one level, today's programmers seem to turn it up yet another notch.

Journalism as Profit Center

Where did all this begin? In my view it started when business analysts in the media industry noticed that news shows actually had listenership and viewership. Until then, news was part of the mix a company was required to present in order to obtain and hold a license to broadcast over the public airwaves. Then the analysts began to see that news could be reshaped into a whole new and lucrative "profit center" capable of pulling down advertising dollars right along with entertainment programming.

Once news programming was cast in this mold, the rest followed naturally: polls were taken to determine what the viewership wanted, extensive analysis of when they tuned in most often, fierce emphasis on "sweeps week," in which more and more strident coverage was unveiled to compete for ratings against other companies. It was no coincidence that vast "exposes" about alleged Satanic cults, racist splinter groups and so forth tended to appear during these super-heated sweeps periods...and more often than not, faded away with no follow up later.

The journalists who labor in the newsrooms of this land don't like these trends any more than other thinking Americans do. No one I have ever met sought a career as a print or broadcast journalist as a road to riches. Almost to a person, they began their careers in idealistic spirits, seeing their role as watchdogs for a free society, reporting the unvarnished truth. Our Founding Fathers believed that government needed a lot of watching—and most reporters believe the same thing, whether it's the local city hall, the county commission, the state house or Congress.

But unless there's a sexual angle anymore—a Speaker cavorting in a reflecting pool with a stripper, say—it's hard for political news to shoulder aside the search for sensationalism. I recall one news director who took over a station with stumbling ratings. This was during one of the many U.S.-led initiatives to try to bring a lasting peace to the war-torn Middle East. The news director's diagnosis of the station's ailing ratings: "too much Reagan and Begin; we need more bleeding and leading!"

And that's exactly what they got.

Stations that try to report news of note—serious news, news that requires perhaps some thought of the listener or viewer—typically wind up third or fourth in the ratings race, beaten by Wheel of Fortune. The force-feeding of information needed for an informed citizenship simply is not popular.

Implications of the 1996 Act

The Communications Act of 1934 obligated broadcast media to serve the public good. That meant radio then, and the obligation was extended to TV when it came into widespread use. But the national trend toward deregulation that culminated in the updated 1996 Act has thrown the door wide open to this blur of market-driven shock-entertainment-news we see today.

Technology has played a significant role in how the media influences our lives. Newspapers were powerfully influential in the days before broadcast. The huge letterpress which enabled daily newspapers to grind out several editions a day were the technology of their era, bringing fresher news to the street faster. When radio first became widespread, the Associated Press, the premier association of newspapers at that time, refused to let its copy be read over the radio.

As radio grew in respectability, it employed "block programming" or blocks of time for entertainment. There would be an orchestra hour, a situation comedy half hour and so forth. Perhaps a half hour of news at 6 and 11 p.m. Wartime brought occasional special programming, but it was the advent of television in the 50s that changed the face of radio.

Entertainment shows decamped wholesale to TV. Radio suddenly was left with just music to play, for the most part. New, briefer formats were chosen to maintain interest and keep dials from being switched. News, typically, moved to ten minutes "at the top of the hour." Given that format and the brevity, the most exciting stuff usually was chosen. This was sort of the genesis of the "if it bleeds, it leads" school. (Though newspapers never lacked for crime coverage over the years, usually breaking the most sensational murders and robberies page one.)

TV news at first followed the old radio format—still does, in some aspects, such as the nightly news broadcasts after work and at 10 or 11—but then radio began to experiment with "news breaks" in their programming instead of waiting for the top of the hour. So TV began experimenting with the same thing.

We began to experience media overload. Remember that old saying, "that's probably more than you wanted to know about that?" Well, in the battle for ratings, which translate into the ability to charge more for commercials, programmers today don't seem to remember it. They seem caught in a never ending round of escalation.

Meanwhile, back on radio, FM appeared, and began to take away AM radio's music. The new hi fidelity stuff, predecessor of stereo, simply sounded lots better on FM. About the only thing AM had left was the non-singing human voice—and Talk Radio began to come into its own. The only music programs left after a while on AM were those aimed at older listeners who couldn't afford an FM radio and wanted to listen to Glen Miller and other wartime favorites.

Now there is Talk Radio. And Talk TV for that matter, scores of "tabloid TV" talk shows concentrating on everything from the sensational to the bizarre.

Media Mergers Detract From the First Amendment

The marketers who control our national media today are almost like another species of humanity, evolved to live entirely in the mechanism of the marketplace with no view beyond it. I have likened them to sharks. Sharks are the sea's perfect eating machine; marketing programmers in the broadcast industry today are the perfect money-making machines, whose only credo is how much money they can churn out of this medium.

I'm far from sure we've reached anything like the peak of this trend.

And I've seen some other trends that are at least equal cause for unease.

Consolidation of the giant media companies is one. A free media always had the implication built in that there would be many voices, and if one news organ chose to ignore a story, another certainly would not. But now with so many news organizations tracing their corporate parentage back up a pyramid to the same board of directors, diversity is threatened. When major international corporations, unanswerable to the people, our nation's government or anyone but shareholders, control a cross-section of our sources of "news," just how objective is that news going to be?

The vast media mergers of 1999 were mostly carried on business pages. And why not? Again, the marketplace, first and last, seems to rule all aspects of American thought. Everything is for sale if the price is right. Even, it could just be, the First Amendment.

We hear an awful lot about "diversity" issues these days when it comes to the workforce and so on. But diversity of ideas, to my mind, is one of the essential underpinnings of freedom. Once we have five or six major media conglomerates whose worth is measured in triple billion digits, there will be an inevitable shrinking of sources of information and viewpoints.

A happy upstart of a publication which, so far as I know, bucks the conglomeratization trend so far is *Brill's Content. Brill's* reports on media issues. It was to *Brill's* I turned to find an example of my concerns about the squeezing down of media coverage where extensive coverage might not be viewed as in the interest of the new media giants.

I mentioned the Telecommunications Act of 1996, which had a greatly deregulating effect on the original 1934 Act. The '96 Act did other things as well. For instance, it set aside a huge chunk of public airwaves for the new digital TV signals. But these airwaves were not auctioned off to the highest bidders, which might have given our government as much as $70 billion to spend for social good, according to *Brill's*.

Under heavy lobbying from the broadcast industry, Congress simply gave the airwaves away.

Don't remember seeing many news exposes about that one, do you?

Brill's quoted U.S. Sen. John McCain, who has established himself as something of an independent thinker, as saying; "You will not see this story on any television or hear it on any radio broadcast because it directly affects them."

Dean Alger & the 1996 Act

A man named Dean Alger analyzed news coverage of the 1996 Act from its introduction to passage, a period of nine months, as reported in his book *Megamedia*. He found a total of 19 1/2 minutes of coverage on the Act, with almost no mention at all of the airwave giveaway.

Of course the broadcasting lobby argued that the gift was justified by their broadcasting in the public interest, but they were then able to defeat a provision that would have called for free airtime for political campaigns.

Consider the ramifications of this move by the broadcast industry in light of my chapter on politics. It's hard for politicians to think seriously about campaign finance reform when the gatekeepers to public acceptance—the media—are charging whatever the rate card will bear for their political ads.

I find it hard to believe the giant media conglomerates are invested in the principles of a participatory democracy, given such a track record. The playing field goes to the well-financed candidate.

Nor were the print media blameless. Dean Alger found that major newspapers, which were part of corporations including broadcast interests, unfailingly threw their editorial support in favor of the airwave giveaway.

Brill's dug up an interview on National Public Radio with the chairman of Disney, in which he said he would prefer that Disney subsidiary ABC News not cover Disney, since "…I think it is inappropriate for Disney to be covered by Disney…" Days later, *Brill's* reports, ABC News killed a story about Disney's unwitting employment of convicted pedophiles in its theme parks.

It seems at least arguable that Big Business has accomplished and will continue to accomplish what Big Brother Government has never been able to do for long in this nation: censor the news.

Two For One Happy Hours

One final example, on a lesser scale—a microcosm if you will—of how such ownership and lobbying can have an effect on issues of public policy which affect all of us. This one goes back a few years, when Mothers Against Drunk Driving (MADD) was a new and vibrant organization, and the public was up in arms nationwide, as it periodically is, about the death toll from drinking and driving.

A state alcohol beverage control agency in the West promulgated administrative rules, which would have the force and effect of law, to ban what was then a common practice: the advertising of "two for one" happy hours during the afternoon commute times. Such advertising was meant to lure drivers out of the traffic and into the watering holes with bargain prices. MADD and others saw such advertising as enticing drivers to drink too much and then drive.

After hearing testimony, the state agency voted unanimously to continue the practice of two-for-one happy hours.

Reporters alerted by MADD called to get the scandalous story firsthand.

Yes, the press was informed, lobbyists did in fact change the agency's mind. But not lobbyists for the liquor industry or the bars. The liquor people were smarter than that. They went to the newspaper publishers' association with figures to show them how much annual advertising revenue they would lose when bars stopped advertising happy hours.

The state agency had no desire to tangle with the representatives of all the state's daily newspapers, who showed up to wave the First Amendment in their faces as a defense for advertising two-fers. Two-for-one happy hours would continue.

Were there banner headlines the next day about newspapers blocking rules to curb drunk driving?

As some comedian once said, "it is to laugh!"

Of course there weren't. And as conglomertization continues, and the "news" we get is decided by marketers pandering to our own worst instincts while carefully protecting their own interests, I truly wonder just where our tradition of freedom of the media will wind up.

Against the monolithic consolidation of giant media in this nation, there is a countervailing trend, stimulated by the availability of hundreds of television channels, and by the ubiquitous Internet. Whether this trend will offer more avenues to unvarnished news I don't know. Internet providers are no less susceptible to merger fever than anyone else, for one thing.

But while all this is shaking out, there will be a dramatic tug of war for the hearts and minds of the nation.

I hope I can be forgiven if I shed a nostalgic tear for the days when the "Big Three" TV companies offered clear alternatives to each other and the whole nation could watch "I Love Lucy." There was a sense of national community, I feel, as we talked next day about Lucille Ball's pregnancy, as it was written into the story line over the course of a season. Even the Super Bowl can't draw Americans together for that sense of shared experience in front of the tube like "Uncle" Milton Berle used to in the innocent early days.

The Internet Assault

While the huge consolidated corporations go the way I've described above, at the other end of the scale, you will be able to isolate yourself as never before to ideas that appeal only to you, and insulate yourself from any discourse with opposing viewpoints. There already are White Supremacy Internet sites where the only discussion is the degree and extent of United Nations conspiracy to absorb the U.S. into an international "state," without any hint that this might be an exaggeration or—perish the thought—simply a myth.

Combine this trend with the power of the marketers, of whom I've already spoken, accept that their single-minded pursuit of ever increasing profits is amoral, and it won't be long, I fear, before you can dial into your very own personal channel via multimedia gadgets that stream TV and radio and Internet all together for your convenience.

If your name is Joe Sixpack, you will sign on to find your very own "Joe" channel awaiting you. Overnight wrestling results, the NASCAR matchups for Saturday and whether the bass are biting this morning on your favorite reservoir. Whatever specific sites you've visited, or channels you've surfed, all ready just for you.

This is an advertiser's dream come true. You select your own preferences as you go along. They have captured them and now feed back to you a mirror image of your own tastes and prejudices daily, reinforcing your sense of self—and oh, by the way, bass boats are on sale right down the street. Yes, the very ones you have looked at on the Internet three times lately. And here's a link to online bass-boat financing!

How does this affect news? Well of course the news items you selected to view also are computerized. Follow-ups to those, and related or similar stories, will be awaiting your click. You won't be troubled by anything you don't want to know about.

Just how likely do you think you will be, given this smorgasbord, to say "No thanks, I'm not sure reinforcing my prejudices every single day is a good idea. I'd like to just get the general news of the world, as selected by someone who may have a different idea of what's important than me?"

I truly believe days like these are just around the corner, and I fear them. So much of what I have thought about and written here is about the downfall of the American ideal, of a community of free citizens, freely joined together, and supporting the concept of life, liberty and the pursuit of happiness for all.

Such downfalls have happened before in history.

The Roman, Juvenal, in his satires, commented: "The people that once bestowed commands, consulships, legions, and all else, now concerns itself no more, and longs eagerly for just two things—bread and circuses!"

Our twenty-first century circuses are Oprah and the Internet, World-wide Wrestling—and Jim Bohannon, some nights. Though some of us still try to make our part of the three-ring circus a place where independent thought can be provoked and welcomed.

We live in an age of technological marvels. We can sit at our computer and chat, as over the back fence, with people all over the world. Will this really give us a global perspective and a sense of friendliness comparable to leaning on the lawnmower at the back corner of our lot? We love to talk, that's for sure. I wouldn't have a job if we didn't.

Maybe the interactive nature of these new media will eventually be harnessed to democratic principles. If they can keep my credit card transactions secure over the net—and the marketers assure us they can—maybe they can in some way ensure one voter, one vote the same way, and democracy will become even quicker and easier than going to the polling place.

Maybe instead of losing your citizenship for not voting, you'll be denied Internet access for ten days. Now there would be a punishment!

Media Creates Misperception

Before I leave this subject of the media, I want to return to the idea I opened with, about the way the media these days seems to pander to a perceived thirst for news of violence in all its forms. Remember when a visitor from out of town was knifed to death on a New York City subway platform? When a deranged gunman opened fire on a commuter train there? Such news makes the Big Apple seem as dangerous as a war zone.

But does anyone pause to think how many millions of commuter and subway passengers go daily about their business without encountering naked steel or gunplay? I have talked to people who feared visiting New York City at all, and particularly riding public transportation, because of the lingering perceptions left by the relatively few violent episodes. They certainly have mistaken news—the unusual—for everyday life in the Big Apple.

And that same misperception seems to pervade the entire country.

The Columbine High School shootings in Colorado were certainly shocking and tragic. The body count was high. Or was it? All around the world outside the United States, within days of that particular episode, if you cared to examine the world's news, scores and hundreds were being killed in various convulsions of religious, political, or tribal hatred. Is Denver as dangerous as the Big Apple now? Is every school as dangerous as Beirut? When serious discussion is being had about metal detectors in grade schools, it makes you wonder.

In this information age of ours, with news of awful things dinned into our minds from every medium, we can well be forgiven for thinking our society is in near-terminal decay. Maybe what we need is a context. I can remember when the late unlamented Soviet Union proclaimed itself a crimeless society. Amazingly enough, there were never any news accounts in the state-run media to contradict that official claim. Did citizens of the Soviet society sleep better for not knowing about serial murderers and other predators who prowled their lands? Let alone all the government corruption which paralyzed their nation? Do we sleep any worse for constantly being told about bad things that happen in ours?

I for one am more concerned in the long run that we're not being told about the behind-the-scenes things, like airwave giveaways and influence on public policy issues. If the media would rededicate itself to examination of all things wrong—including the things wrong about its own house—I could put up with all the blood and gore with a little better attitude.

The Fourth Estate

This is a weighty issue for me. I have spent most of my adult life in some form of news gathering or media work. A free press is one of the basic tenets of my beliefs about things. Our Founding Fathers put "the fourth estate" into our Bill of Rights for a reason: to perform as a watchdog for the people. Remember: Washington and Franklin and Jefferson, et al, may be hallowed figures to us—but to King George they were rebels. They chose to institutionalize their distrust of high-handed government in our most sacred document. If corporations had been as all-powerful then as they are now—essentially stateless empires of their own—I have no doubt the Founding Fathers would have included them as worthy of healthy skepticism.

It may take contemporary wisdom as powerful as that of our Founders to figure out how to deal with a media grown so wealthy and pervasive that is shapes our entire view of ourselves and our land. Because in the end, these mega-companies answer only to their stockholders, and not to we, the people.

CHAPTER 13

Twelve Step Program for America

THROUGHOUT THIS BOOK, I HOPE I HAVE RAISED QUESTIONS, provided food for thought, maybe even been a little provocative. Okay, a lot provocative in some things. I am a great believer in discourse and debate. Man is a political animal. When you boil politics right down to its basics, politics is all about talk and debate. About persuasion and conviction and compromise.

In this country, such discourse has been defined as a free and open marketplace of ideas. Each debater putting forward his or her views, to be accepted or rejected, or accepted partially, by others. Unfortunately I think the "marketplace of ideas" concept, originally noble, has been blurred by the ascendance in our nation of the actual marketplace, where ideas are bought and sold for cash value received. Politicians are for sale, justice is for sale—heck, just about everything is for sale.

That's not what America was meant to be about.

Before I leave this topic, I want to make it clear that I am not against the actual marketplace. I believe history will show that the advent of trade was one of the first truly civilizing influences on our species.

History shows that humankind has lived longer in insular tribes than in civilized communities. I have a hunch that tribal mentality lies not too far beneath our surface veneer of civilization. Nationalism, like feudalism before it, may just be an extension of tribal mentality.

When two roving bands of hunter-gatherers found happy hunting grounds in prehistoric times, they tended to have at each other until one tribe quit the field, or was demolished. Even by the time that stone-age cultures, like our American Indians before the arrival of Europeans, had kind of sorted out territorial imperatives, there was raiding and warfare on each other. Tribe over the hill has horses? We take horses. (Granted, the horses weren't there to take until Europeans arrived, and the Apaches stole the first ones from the Spaniards. But to the Apaches, the Spanish were just another tribe.) Tribe down the valley has women we need? We take women.

In our inner city ghettos, where civilization is stripped away by despair and poverty, we see kid gangs revert to this tribal pattern. Store (or unaffiliated kid) has fancy sneakers? We take sneakers. Loyalty is to the tribe, or gang. Gang "colors" are like warpaint. Turf wars over street corners and drug-delivery routes supplant hunting-grounds clashes. But the parallels are striking.

In every stone age, from the ancient ones in China to the European stone age, to the first Americans, trade appeared at some point in the proceedings. Some bucolic creative thinker decided it made more sense to exchange maize for pelts, or salmon for buffalo jerky, than to try stealing it. Again, looking at our own continent, at least two spoken linguas franca developed so that tribes with widely varying languages could barter. And the immemorial sign language was a third method of communication and trade.

Roving traders like the Phoenicians spread culture and new developments all around the Mediterranean. Along fertile river valleys like the Nile, grand civilizations arose. There still was plenty of warfare, but trade provided more opportunities for wealth than conquest did, in the long run. In a way, Japan is a modern-day example. Their militaristic efforts to seize oil fields in order to fuel their burgeoning pre-war empire led to them making mistakes like Pearl Harbor.

Out of the ruins of their demolished imperial dreams, they turned to trade instead of bayonets, and climbed to financial preeminence among nations.

Our exuberant economy, from high priced sneakers to sport utility vehicles costing as much as houses did 20 years ago, is the lineal descendant of trading woven goods for pelts, maize for venison, smoked salmon for buffalo. Business, which nobility used to condescend to as the "merchant class," has achieved preeminence.

All well and good. It sure beats living in a windowless log cabin with rifle loopholes on every wall. (Though living in a triple-deadbolt ghetto apartment may be about the same thing.) Our free-market economy is just fine.

But it is not and should not be the only or even the main driving force in the United States of America.

Life and liberty, truth and justice for all. These are the kinds of things we need to work on. And we need to start now.

Democracy, I believe, is like a close friendship. You develop a close friendship, the two of you enjoy each other's company enormously, and always manage to find time out of your busy schedules to keep the friendship green. Then something happens—one moves away, or work becomes all-demanding, or family. The friendship lies fallow, though in your mind you still see it just as it was. Maybe a good period of time goes by, and one day you pick up the phone out of the blue and call your friend, fully expecting to slide back into the warm natural rhythm of two minds in synch on many things.

Instead…there are pauses, breaks in the conversation. Cordiality, sure, but something is missing. You have not nurtured the relationship, and it has withered.

Democracy, I truly believe, is like that.

If you do not nurture it, do not participate fully as a citizen, it withers. I think our democracy has withered and is withering, largely due to apathy and neglect on the part of its citizens.

So to conclude my thoughts on the crises facing the U.S., I would like to put forward my own modest 12-step plan to bring America back on track. Some of these steps we can do immediately, and some will take significant commitment over time to achieve. Perhaps I am proposing a democratic version of Utopia. But here is what I think we need to do.

Soon!

MY TWELVE STEPS FOR AMERICA

1) Vote!

Your vote lies at the bedrock of our system of government. Vote in all national and local elections. Inform yourself on the candidates and issues. I am sick and tired of people telling me it's too much trouble to vote.

It's about as much trouble to go to the polling place as it is to run to the store for microwave popcorn before the Game of the Week. But sometimes I think more people do the latter than the former.

I take my vote seriously. I get the pamphlets published by neutral organizations like the League of Women Voters, which give brief sketches of each politician and their positions, and of each school levy or initiative measure. On the latter, they provide the legalese first and then say in English what the legalese would do.

Even taking my vote seriously, going through the pamphlet and ascribing a number value of 0-100 to each candidate and issue and then adding up the totals, I have never spent more than an hour and a half preparing myself to vote. And that length of time only when it was a presidential year, plus federal Congress positions, state and local offices, and a good number of ballot issues.

Even if you spent an hour and half every year informing yourself and voting on everything from school boards to fire districts—is that so much to ask?

If you think so, shame on you.

I once editorialized on my radio show, saying "thanks for not voting," talking to those who couldn't be bothered. Telling them their absence permitted the votes of those who did bother to have more weight. I'm afraid that was my own descent to cynicism. I'd much rather see voting be an obligation of citizenship instead of an option.

In this technological age, our failure to vote could be linked to Internal Revenue Service computers. Don't vote this year, lose your automatic individual tax exemption. I'd love to see that put on a ballot as an initiative! I bet that would get the vote out! Once, anyway. If it didn't, the rest of us would perhaps see our tax burdens eased when Uncle Sugar started collecting all that extra income tax from the non-voting.

If the stick doesn't appeal to you, why not a carrot?

Perhaps an additional tax exemption could be offered if you do vote. Almost everyone I've ever known is always looking for deductions to lower their tax bite. I have always believed that taxes serve not only as a revenue source, but also as a method to nudge citizens into appropriate behavior. So a tax incentive to vote would accomplish that.

I noted not too long ago that the State of Oregon conducted a mail-in vote as an experiment. The results were pretty amazing. In elections where normal turnouts had been about a quarter of the electorate, the vote percentage doubled to almost 50 percent. Just because it was easier to vote!

Perhaps a combined mail-in and Internet-link election would push those numbers even higher. If making it easier to vote is all it takes (though I still don't see that going to the polls is that big a deal) then by all means let's make it easier.

Another incentive might be to put the initiative vote-gathering process on the Internet, along with election voting. Initiatives by the people seem to be enjoying a vogue among voters who don't think their representatives listen to them anymore. The hardest part of acquiring a ballot spot is gathering the signatures of registered voters. Sign up sheets on business counters or card tables in front of the super market, require vast numbers of volunteers and organization. If we made signing onto an initiative as easy as web-surfing, voters could begin to see their will manifested more readily. And politicians would by golly take rapid notice, and pay more attention, when they knew initiatives could be launched more readily.

My recommended first step is directed both to you, the individual voter, and to government. To you: vote! To the government, make voting more attractive, whatever it takes.

2) Help Stamp Out Apathy and Cynicism

In our society today, apathy and cynicism are the evil twins. There seems to be a nationwide malaise that convinces us that nothing we can do or say will make a difference. So we don't vote, we don't join volunteer groups, we don't write letters to Congress or the state legislature or city hall or the news media. We seem to feel no one cares what we think.

I know that this malaise does not infect us all. There are many fine service organizations and church groups that do amazing work for the less fortunate, and truly do make a difference. There are hundreds of thousands of dedicated professionals who make it their life's work to serve, from nurses to police officers to unsung civil servants.

But so many of us work just for a paycheck, and the work seems to exhaust all our reserves. We vainly pursue more and better toys, more exotic vacations, and we pretty much let the world go by. Some of this may be admirable—an endearing trait of Americans is to mind our own business—but the business of this nation IS our business.

Apathy—the feeling that nothing we do or say will have a positive effect—leads to lazy thinking, and to cynicism. When I espoused the need for more critical thinking skills recently, a very well read friend protested, "but everyone is so critical of everything!" She was using the word in the sense of negative criticism—or cynicism!

Even the language seems to have been corrupted.

The ability to think critically means to consider and weigh arguments and issues, and form our own opinions, upon which we then can act. An informed citizenry is the first defense against demagogues and extremists of all stripes. You consider all points of view and make your own decisions.

If you just don't take the time to bother, events will certainly roll on without your input. Your apathetic approach can lead to a weary cynicism: "they're going to do what they want to do anyway." Such lazy thinking is reflected in an almost unanimous distrust of politicians, of the media, of government, of institutions in general.

Politicians and reporters are human, the government and institutions are shaped by humans, and by far the majority of them are doing what they consider the best they can. If what they are doing doesn't square with your ideas, how are they ever going to know that unless you speak up? How are you ever going to know what they're trying to accomplish in the first place if you don't inform yourself?

I find myself resorting to ancient axioms as I consider the state of affairs in our nation. As Edmund Burke noted, "All that is necessary for the triumph of evil is that good men do nothing."

Our nation and its institutions need your thoughts, your input, even (perhaps especially) your dissent. I am not suggesting you automatically take a position diametrically opposed to whatever spectrum you are observing. Rather that you take the time to look critically at events and their shapers and make your voice heard. You may agree that a particular problem is pressing, but may completely disagree with the methods being employed to address it. Nobody's going to know unless you speak up.

I said above that citizenship requires nurturing. In our democracy, we the people are designated as the ruling class. If we surrender to the evil twins of apathy and cynicism, and focus solely on our hedonist pursuit of jacuzzis and summer homes, we become the equivalent of notorious Nero, the ruler who fiddled while Rome burned.

America's not burning, thank God. Not just yet. But I do smell smoke.

Get off your butt and start making a difference! Whether by becoming a Big Brother or Sister, coaching little league, or writing your elected officials. Do something!

3) Compromise Is Not a Dirty Word!

I am so very tired of extremism in all forms. From the left, from the right; from the pro-abortionists, from the anti-abortionists; from the pro-gunners, from the anti-gunners. When did compromise become a dirty word? It seems that every issue must be supercharged with distrust, fear and yes, even hate. I think that's very sad, and very un-American. Some of our greatest leaders were great compromisers, who could find a middle way through violently contending factions. Could strike compromises that would ensure each faction received some of their most important concessions, and surrendered others.

The U.S. Supreme Court, in a landmark ruling, upheld the premise of one person, one vote. This was meant to disassemble a situation where certain wealthy districts could have a disproportionate influence on elected bodies. But redistricting is a legislative, not a judicial function. Political parties, when they have the majority of votes, have been redistricting to protect themselves ever since the media coined the term "gerrymandering." (On the map, a redrawn political district meant to ensure re-election on one party's candidates resembled a salamander sprawling around pockets of the other party's voters. And the term gerrymandering was coined. To give this word a place in history, one of the delegates to the Constitution and later the vice president to James Madison, Elbridge Gerry, was at the time of this word coming into existence (1812) the governor of Massachusetts. After Governor Gerry passed a measure ensuring the victory of his party, the Federalists ridiculed him and attached his name to the front of a new word.)

Political parties remain uncomfortable with districts where a candidate might win his or her seat with something like a 55-45 percent vote total. Hardly a mandate. That representative goes to work realizing 45 percent of the constituency was not impressed. How to increase the margin next time? Listen to some of the issues the 45 percent consider important while attending to the things the 55 percent want to see accomplished.

Which spells compromise in my book.

But political parties are like horse handicappers: they want their nag to have the weight advantage. If redistricting gives them a pool of voters who will come down 70-30 or 80-20 for their candidate, the troublesome chore of seeking a middle path is eliminated. Let some other candidate worry about those other voters, is the view of someone elected from such a lopsided district. You can always deadlock that vote with your own. I realize that districts with fewer wasted votes more closely represent what may be seen as the majority view, but we are far better served by districts which elect politicians forced to consider all viewpoints. In short, in this case, less representation is better representation.

And thus Congress, for one, spends a lot of time in gridlock, instead of finding reasonable compromises on programs that can help pull America out of its doldrums and get it moving again as an idealistic, can-do nation.

4) Turn Down The Volume!

Most of my adult career has been financed by advertising sales. Producers of goods and services have a perfect right to contend for our dollars in the open marketplace. But enough, already!

Advertising whose net effect is to render miserable whole segments of our population who cannot afford the wares advertised is not in this nation's best interest. Cunning language and special effects which suggest you are less than a whole person without this or that gadget borders on the immoral.

At the worst end of the scale fall those "sweepstakes" advertising scams that prey on the elderly and the weak-minded. Recently, I became aware of the horrible consequences that sometimes follow an addiction to "home-buying network" programs. Lonely older Americans find themselves being cajoled and cuddled by the sales forces, made to feel special in return for reciting their credit card numbers over the phone. There are cases on record of fixed-income widows running up tens of thousands of dollars in credit-card debt. That's despicable.

To hide behind freedom-of-commercial speech and *caveat emptor* (let the buyer beware) doctrine is preposterous.

While older Americans are susceptible to feel-good marketing, our youth seem mesmerized by the Pied Piper allure of designer jeans, cell phones, video games and cool cars. If you don't have those things, you're just not with it.

Some credit-card companies cynically target young collegians, out from under the family roof for the first time in their lives. Put it on plastic is the name of the game. There is an upsurge of young college-age individuals who must seek consumer-credit counseling to deal with the debt they accrued so easily with the new plastic. In some cases, the veteran counselors have to tell the applicants that their starting-job income is too low to even cover a consolidated debt repayment plan.

It is all well and good to say we are free to make our own choices, and it's our individual responsibility to keep track of and satisfy our debts. But the siren voices are all around us, full volume, with very little in the way of countervailing caution to alert us that all is not so rosy. The exhortations to buy, buy, buy, drown out the voices of reason.

Maybe it's time for warning labels on advertising: "Warning: too much purchase on plastic can leave you homeless under a bridge abutment."

5) Raising Children Is Not a Part-Time Hobby

I have addressed this in the family, school and poverty chapters. I am convinced we need some kind of financial-responsibility training of those who would be parents. In addition to being able to afford to feed the extra mouths, there must be serious and long-lasting commitment to and knowledge how to go about raising them to adulthood.

Keeping up with the Joneses in terms of purchasing new cars and VCRs is not the commitment I am talking about. I mean reading to them, nurturing them, being there for them when the world skins their knees.

6) If Families Won't Do It, Society Must

We can bemoan the fact that children today haven't had the advantage of a traditional family to instill independent thinking skills and a sense of personal self esteem and values all we want. But the fact is, hundreds of thousands of them are pretty much growing up like weeds, often in a toxic environment.

Children having children is a serious problem today. I don't think high school kids should be allowed to graduate without a minimum of one semester on the realities and responsibilities of parenting and marriage. The war over sex education was a long and hard one, and still is being waged. We need to sit aside our prejudices and cherished presumptions, and lay out in no uncertain terms for our young people the consequences of pregnancy and parenthood.

And yes, I think we need to consider some serious interventionist steps to curtail the problem. Children need structure in their lives. Perhaps we need to consider boarding schools for children from shattered and dysfunctional families, where social skills and interpersonal relationships are taught right along with the three Rs.

We definitely need to define what a "good" education is, to include training in how to be a citizen, a neighbor, a parent. How can a young person know what it means to be a good parent if she or he has never even seen one?

It is society's responsibility to step in and provide training that families have failed to give. Our schools will have to be the instrument of that training. In my view, the importance of such training is at least on a par with literacy: what good is a generation of young barbarians who can read? So they can read the name of your home security company on the window sticker before they cut the phone line to break in?

For the rowdiest and most unruly of our youth, I like the idea of "boot camps" to impose structure on their lives. This was a good idea whose popularity has waned. There was a time early in the twentieth century when judges would sometimes offer a delinquent a choice between jail time and enlistment in the military. Those who chose the latter usually came out of the experience far better for it, solid citizens. Maybe it's time to look at some of that wisdom of the past, as military enrollment dwindles with no compulsory draft to drive it.

7) When It Comes To Good Government, There Is No Free Lunch

Waging a successful war on poverty, reshaping our schools to make up for the deficiencies of today's fragmented families, redesigning our voting system to ensure high turnouts—none of these things will come without a significant cost in dollars.

Taxes are not popular with anyone, never have been.

But taxes are the way we finance the society we want. The fact is, we have to make unhappy choices about how to spend the taxes we can afford to have levied on us.

We need to involve ourselves with the Congress and the state houses which shape our governmental budgets, and insist on the redirection of priorities to the things that will set our society aright. We need to stop whining about the high cost of civil servants' salaries (they really aren't all that high) and ensure that the civil service is engaged in the work we want: rebuilding our nation. Our nation has, by the way, one of the lowest tax burdens in the entire developed world.

And we need to demand that a balanced budget is kept at the same time, which means some issues will take time to address. That's where difficult choices come in. How can we expect our families to stay out of debt when our nation can't? The government needs to set the example.

I understand there needs to be flexibility here, in case of emergent needs. A threat to our national security might be one, though that has been done to death over the years by military brass and the military-industrial complex of lobbyists. But we must require a really high threshold of proof before deficit spending is allowed.

When periods of prosperity arrive, as in the late 90s and the early part of this century, we need to require that the surplus be carefully husbanded. At last report, as I was writing, there was a significant national surplus. True to form, Democratic leaders wanted to spend it on new government programs, and Republicans wanted to return it to taxpayers in the form of tax breaks. Either position has been a sure-fire vote getter for certain constituencies.

Which is where those critical thinking skills that I keep harping on come in. Think about it: would you rather have a new federal program in your neighborhood, or a few more dollars in your paycheck, or a nation with a surplus that is gaining interest against the day when some real threat or need might materialize?

8) We Must Rethink Victimless Crime

Human beings will accept government when it gives them a sense of order and security in their lives. Oftentimes those in power find their efforts blurring over into the category of attempting to regulate things that are perceived to be in the people's own interest—whether the people agree or not. This is never more apparent than in the "victimless crimes" category.

The "unholy three" of drugs (including alcohol), gambling and prostitution have absorbed incredible amounts of our national energy in attempts to suppress such activities. The reason it takes so much energy is that an awful lot of people don't choose to be suppressed. We need to consider what's at stake in each case and proceed accordingly.

It isn't enough to just legalize all three on the principle that the state can't regulate morality. Laws, by definition, often attempt to do just that.

The difference is that where clear victims exist, there's a greater consensus in support of prohibition and punishment; for instance, activities like murder, rape, and robbery. For the "unholy three" we have to decide what the state can and should do. I think we can distinguish between gambling, prostitution, and some drugs on the one hand, and harder drugs on the other.

The suffering caused by addiction to drugs such as heroin and cocaine is real. Further, society has absolutely no vested interest in subsidizing zombies, unfit for any productive purpose. However, as the "Noble Experiment" proved, the law can only go so far in nudging people's behavior. While a zealous minority forced the nation into legal abstinence because of their concern with the (very genuine) harm which can be caused by excessive alcohol intake, there was such a huge group in opposition that the result was disrespect for the law. The market for booze was there, and a huge criminal enterprise grew up to serve it. Every drinker became a scofflaw, and respect for all law suffered. Even the President of the United States, Warren Harding, our nation's top law enforcement officer, had a stash of booze in the White House. There's very little to recommend consumption of alcohol, past a few studies indicating a glass of wine now and then may help the heart. But there's nothing to recommend laws that completely defy public acceptance.

So we have legal alcohol again. What about the rest of the drugs? The use of, and acceptance of, cocaine, LSD, and heroin, to name just a few, isn't nearly as high. But it is high enough to fuel a huge criminal enterprise which places many in our society at risk from its secondary effects, such as addicts committing crimes to support their habits. One has to consider whether duly regulated dissemination to the incurable addict might not save untold corollary suffering of others.

As for marijuana, it may well have crossed the line into the too-accepted-for-prohibition category, in which case decriminalization should proceed. Marijuana could be regulated like liquor is now, freeing up thousands of police, prosecutors and judges for more productive work, just at the Repeal of Prohibition did.

Gambling also has its addictive qualities, but there's little the state can do other than regulate how much one can legally gamble, and try to put the squeeze on illegal gambling. But, like drugs, if there is a market for illegal games of chance, there will be an outlaw enterprise to supply the demand. Limits on legal gambling are simple enough in this computer age. Simply enact laws which say people may only partake of state lotteries, etc. up to a given percentage of their gross income as reflected on a their last income tax filing. As a side benefit, no tax filing, no gambling allowed. Computers could easily keep track of how much a person had wagered in a given year and after you hit the limit, forget it till next January.

As for prostitution, no amount of laws ever has put a dint in the world's oldest profession. Prostitution is another of those enterprises that will be (and presently is) entirely in criminal hands if outlawed. Arguments that existence of prostitutes threaten family stability fall down, since prostitutes exist anyway. I hardly think it likely that its legalization would destroy the family. Put bluntly, sex is available enough in our society. The only real harm from prostitution comes from its UN-regulation (that is, the lack of order, which is the one thing government can offer its people) which results in abuse of prostitutes by pimps, vicious working conditions and disease. Legalized and properly regulated, so that only those who truly chose this profession operated in it, and operated safely under the protection of the law, this would truly be the most victimless of crimes.

9) Justice For All

Our criminal justice system is in sad need of overhaul. I don't like the thought of prosecutors and district attorneys building a track record of successful prosecutions against the indigent, the working poor, and the middle class, because none of these groups can afford adequate legal representation. On the other hand, real crime, economic or violent, or both, must never be permitted to pay.

Through active participation in the voting process, we must elect public prosecutors and DAs who will go after the real predators in our society: organized crime figures, professional burglars and robbers, habitual rapists and assaulters. They need to go after the white collar criminal too, the one who steals your identity through computer fraud, or cons the unsuspecting out of their hard-earned dollars.

I like the three-strikes-and-out approach for hardened criminals. If they can't rehabilitate themselves after two bites of the apple, they're not likely to do it at all. I don't think such toughness will require a huge outlay for new prisons, if other reforms I have talked about come into play. But even if incarceration costs go up, costs in personal economic loss and suffering to our citizenry will go down. I consider that a fair trade-off.

10) Money Is Not The Only Thing That Matters

Far too many of us spend most of our productive years chasing after and worshipping the Almighty Dollar. I know that for many fathers and mothers, two incomes are a necessity just to provide the basics of food and shelter. Housing costs are prohibitive in many parts of the nation.

But we need to re-evaluate how much is enough. If we are going to raise families, and live a life worth living, we will have to ask ourselves some hard questions.

Do the kids really need a car just because they're old enough to drive? Do we really need a ski boat, jacuzzi, motorhome? Aren't generic blue jeans just as sturdy as the designer kind? Homecooked meals are more nutritious and cheaper than even a trip to the Golden Arches. Our supermarkets offer an international cornucopia that would daze those from other lands.

We need to refocus on what a good life means. Money is a necessary part of it, but by no means the end-all and be-all. Far too many well-off and even wealthy families are as emotionally bereft as those struggling in penury. Money isn't the final answer.

11) Money Has Its Uses

I recently read a whimsical column that reflected on the sheer audacity of whoever dreamed up money to start with: talk about abstract notions! Exchanging polished shells or bits of metal or paper for things of real value like land and food. What a concept!

Money is just that, a concept. A mechanism for trade. We trade the sweat of our brow and brains for a concept called "money" and then we exchange our stash of that concept for things needed or wanted.

As a medium of exchange, money has its uses. Instead of lavishing it on our kids, for example, we could reestablish a rewards system. So many bucks per 'A' on the report card, for instance, or for mowing the lawn. We can learn to budget the stuff, harnessing its power to what we really want or need.

12) A Good Education Is The Most Important Gift a Society Can Offer The Individual

This may sound repetitive, but I remain convinced of its truth. That said, I have offered some suggestions here and there about how to enhance that education for our young people. Society must step in where families have failed. Life skills and parenting skills, vocational training and training in how to deal with a complex modern society, from income tax to insurance, should be offered and given the same weight as the basics of reading, writing and arithmetic.

It was once widely held that a "classical" education, exposure to all the great thinkers of history, to art, to science, to the humanities, would prepare a student fully to deal with life. Someone once said that an effective society must have good plumbers as well as philosophers. I firmly subscribe to that view. Exposing students to the complexities of modern life in a classroom environment, with knowledgeable teachers present, will go a long way toward helping them become effective citizens and well-rounded individuals.

A democracy whose majority of voters have been offered these gifts will be a nation that can survive and thrive in the coming challenges of this new century.

Suggested Reading

Incivility

Carnegie, Dale. *How to Win Friends & Influence People*. New York, NY: Pocket Books, 1982.

Charles, C. Leslie. *Why Is Everyone So Cranky?: The Ten Trends That Are Making Us Angry and How We Can Find Peace of Mind Instead*. New York, NY: Hyperion, 1999.

Gibbon, Edward. *History of the Decline and Fall of the Roman Empire*. New York, NY: Modern Library, 1995.

U.S. News & World Report, "I'm Okay, You're Not: Why Americans Think Their Life is Good, But the Nation Is in Peril," Dec. 16, 1996.

Washington, George. *George Washington's Rules of Civility and Decent Behavior in Company and Conversation*. Bedford, MA: Applewood Books, 1994.

Dumbing Down

Calkins, Lucy McCormick. *Raising Lifelong Learners: A Parent's Guide*. New York, NY: Perseus Press, 1998.

Hunter, James Davison. *The Death of Character: Moral Education in an Age Without Good or Evil*. New York, NY: Basic Books, 2000.

Hewlitt, Sylvia Ann. *When the Bough Breaks: The Cost of Neglecting Our Children*. New York, NY: Basic Books, 1991.

Macaulay, David. *The New Way Things Work*. New York, NY: Houghton Mifflin Co., 1998.

Stout, Maureen. *The Feel-Good Curriculum: The Dumbing Down of America's Kids in the Name of Self-Esteem*. New York, NY: Perseus Press, 2000.

Victimless Crime

McWilliams, Peter. *Ain't Nobody's Business If You Do: The Absurdity of Consensual Crimes in Our Free Country*. Los Angeles, CA: Prelude Press, 1995.

Selfishness

Putnam, Robert. *Bowling Alone: The Collapse and Revival of American Community*. New York, NY: Simon & Schuster, 2000.

Schor, Juliet. *The Overspent American: Upscaling, Downshifting and the New Consumer*. New York, NY: Harper Collins, 1999.

Dirt Roads and Lost Identity

Castells, Manuel. *The Rise of the Network Society*. Oxford, UK: Blackwell Publishers, 1996.

_____. *The Power of Identity: The Information Age — Economy, Society and Culture*. Oxford, UK: Blackwell Publishers, 1997.

_____. *End of Millennium*. Oxford, UK: Blackwell Publishers, 1998.

Apathy

Eliasoph, Nina. *Avoiding Politics: How Americans Produce Apathy in Everyday Life*. Boston, MA: Cambridge University Press, 1998.

Rosenthal, A.M. *Thirty-Eight Witnesses: The Kitty Genovese Case*. Berkeley, CA: University of California Press, 1999.

Thau, Richard & Heflin, Jay. *Generations Apart: Xers vs. Boomers vs. the Elderly*. New York, NY: Prometheus Books, 1997.

Themba, Makani. *Making Policy, Making Change: How Communities Are Taking Laws Into Their Own Hands.* Oakland, CA: Chardon Press, 1999.

Family

Doiron, Devra. *Well-Behaved Children: 100 Tips From Parents Who Have Them.* Australia: Seaview Press, 2000.

Zero Population Growth web site: www.zpg.org. Dedicated to saving the world for our children.

Poverty

Harrison, Lawrence & Huntington, Samuel. *Culture Matters: How Values Shape Human Progress.* New York, NY: Basic Books, 2000.

Landes, David. *The Wealth & Poverty of Nations: Why Some are So Rich and Some so Poor.* New York, NY: W.W. Norton & Company, 1999.

Politics

Eberly, Don. *America's Promise: Civil Society and the Renewal of American Culture.* Lanham, MD: Rowman & Littlefield, 1998.

Gross, Martin Louis. *The End of Sanity: Social and Cultural Madness in America.* New York, NY: Avon Books, 1998.

Lapham, Lewis. *Waiting for the Barbarians.* New York, NY: Verso, 1997.

The National Journal. Subscriptions available through web site: http://nationaljournal.com or at 202-739-8400.

Novak, Robert. *Completing the Revolution: A Vision for Victory in 2000.* New York, NY: Free Press, 2000.

Foreign Policy

Ambrose, Stephen. *Rise to Globalism: American Foreign Policy Since 1938.* New York, NY: Penguin USA, 1993.

Lind, Michael. *Vietnam the Necessary War: A Reinterpretation of America's Most Disastrous Military Conflict.* New York, NY: Free Press, 1999.

Sorley, Lewis. *A Better War: The Unexamined Victories and the Final Tragedy of America's Last Years in Vietnam*. New York, NY: Harcourt Brace, 1999.

Crime and Punishment

Currie, Elliott. *Crime and Punishment in America*. New York, NY: Owl Books, 1998.

The Media

Kerbel, Matthew. *If It Bleeds, It Leads: An Anatomy of Television News*. Boulder, CO: Westview Press, 2000.

Parenti, Michael. *Dirty Truths: Reflections on Politics, Media, Ideology, Conspiracy, Ethnic Life and Class Power*. San Francisco, CA: City Lights Books, 1996.

General Interest

The American Enterprise: A National Magazine of Politics, Business, and Culture. Subscriptions available through their web site: www.theamericanenterprise.org or at 888-295-9007.

Harper's Magazine. Subscriptions available through their web site: www.harpers.org or at 800-444-4653.

The Atlantic Monthly. Subscriptions available through their web site: www.theatlantic.com or at 800-234-2411.

Index

C

campaign finance reform 87,
93-94, 97, 129

capitalism 102, 106, 107

Carlin, George 59

Castro, Fidel 80, 107

children 12, 15, 19, 20, 21, 23,
24, 25, 26, 27, 29, 30, 31, 61,
67, 68, 70, 71, 72, 73, 74, 75, 76,
78, 79, 81, 82, 83, 85, 117, 119,
145, 146, 153
children having children 146

China 25, 103, 104, 110, 138

citizen 24, 25, 29, 31, 34, 37, 39,
54, 57, 62, 63, 64, 65, 66, 67, 68,
71, 76, 82, 93, 110, 121, 132,
134, 139, 146, 147, 152

citizenry 90, 115, 142, 150

citizenship 25, 31, 46, 126, 133,
140, 143

civil liberties 118

civil rights 61, 64, 112
Civil Rights Movement 70

Civil War, the 67, 70, 71, 93

civility 11, 13, 14, 15, 16, 17,
18, 53, 64, 153
U.S. News & World Report poll
16

Clinton, Bill 16, 37

Cold War, the 70, 71, 85, 103,
106

Columbine High School massacre
30, 133

Communism 102, 106

communists 85, 102, 103, 106,
108, 109, 110, 111

community 30, 36, 43, 51, 65,
83, 84, 85, 86, 131, 132, 154
sense of 46, 47, 49, 50, 63

compromise 59, 60, 137, 143-144

Congress 35, 56, 81, 85, 86, 88,
89, 90, 92, 95, 126, 129, 140,
141, 144, 147

Congress of Industrial Organizations 94

Constitution, the 35, 63, 67, 87,
101, 104, 144

consumer society 22

contemplation, fear of 47

crack 20, 22, 38, 83

credit 28, 56, 133, 145
living on 79

crime 33-43, 53, 82, 83, 84, 86,
115-121, 127, 134, 150
crime statistics 115
drug-related 36, 39, 83
organized crime 34, 35,
42, 150
punishment, crime and
115-121, 156
victimless crime 42, 118,
148, 154

Crockett, Davy 45

Cronkite, Walter 111

cyberspace 51

cybersquatting 57
Anticybersquatting Consumer
Protection Act 57

cynicism 92, 140, 141, 142, 143

D

de Tocqueville, Alexis 47, 49, 101

death penalty 116, 117, 119, 120

decency 11

Declaration of Independence 104

*History of the Decline and Fall of
the Roman Empire, The* 14, 153

Delinquency Areas 83

democracy 26, 62, 64, 88, 90,
93, 102, 103, 104, 106, 109,
125, 129, 133, 143, 152
defined 139

T

talk radio 127, 128

teachers 26, 30, 31, 101
  excellent 26, 27-28, 31
  frustrated 20
  merit pay of 26

teaching 19, 20, 21, 25, 26, 27,
  28, 31, 36, 49, 64, 80, 82, 84

television 19, 23, 50, 89, 105,
  127, 129, 131, 156

Temperance Movement 35, 36

test score results 27

Tet Offensive 7, 111

30-somethings 60

Thompson, C. B. 101

Twain, Mark 64, 65

Twelve Step Program for America
  137-152

V

Ventura, Jesse "The Body" 62

Vietnam War 7, 19, 23, 70, 78,
  86, 108-109, 110, 111, 112, 155,
  156

violence 18, 23, 30, 38, 41, 83,
  86, 102, 123
  in the media 22, 23, 30, 124,
  133

vocational training 27, 31, 151

Volstead, Andrew J. 35

voting 20, 21, 25, 26, 35, 46, 56,
  63, 67, 80, 88, 89, 90, 91, 92, 94,
  95, 96, 97, 98, 100, 109, 112,
  133, 140-141, 143, 144, 147,
  148, 150, 152

W

war on poverty 80-82, 84, 85,
  147

Washington D.C. 1, 7, 8, 91

Washington, George 94, 95, 101,
  134, 153

Watergate 61, 93

When the Bough Breaks 23

white supremacy 131

work ethic 22

World War One 34, 106

World War Two 83, 103, 106,
  108

worldsexguide.org 41

X

"X" generation 61

Y

"Y" generation 61

The Official Jim Bohannon Newsletter

Stay up-to-date and dig deeper into Jim Bohannon's views on the issues with the new Bohannon Letter.

Jim Bohannon's official newsletter offers his views on the most current events as well as exploring the issues he has always cared about — the state of our nation and what we can do to honestly make it a country to be proud of. Jim addresses the hard questions, challenges his listeners and readers to look for and act on their answers.

Jim also highlights his guests, lets you know about his scheduled appearances, and reviews the month's news.

Ordering Information

To subscribe, contact Paper Chase Press at **800.864.7991**

Or you may send check or money order for $39.95 to

The Bohannon Letter
Paper Chase Press
8175 S Virginia Street, Suite 850
Reno, NV 89511

CHECK OUT

Jimbotalk.com

THE OFFICIAL JIM BOHANNON WEBSITE

FOR

- Jim's take on current events
- Guest Information, Schedule
- Jim's favorite links
- Schedule of Jim's Events and Appearances
- Updated photos of Jim and guests
- Excerpts from *The Bohannon Letter*

AND MORE, MORE, MORE...